HORROR FLICK

— A Novel —

Bob Zeidman

Swiss Creek Publications

Cupertino, CA

ISBN 978-0970227607

10   9   8   7   6   5   4   3   2

Book design by Carrie Zeidman

Printed in the United States of America

Chapter 1

"How about *The Beast From Twenty Thousand Fathoms*?"

"No." Charlotte drags out the vowel for sarcastic emphasis, her cherry lips forming a near-perfect circle. She ambles further down the aisle, black stiletto heals clicking against white tile floor, tight black skirt swaying with the well-rehearsed see-saw motion of her rear end. "How about *Love Story*?"

"*Love Story*? Yuck. Ever see *Blood Beach*?" Stu doesn't look up, but holds the video box up in her direction, shaking it like a tambourine. He expects to get a veto on this choice. His eyes move slowly, methodically, across each row to the end, then zipping to the beginning of the next like the carriage of an old typewriter, not missing a single title.

"How can you watch that stuff?" Charlotte continues walking, her right index finger sliding across each and every box in the top row as if she could read the titles with her fingertips. Her eyes randomly survey the cassettes on the shelves, up and down, left and right, circling and backtracking in no particular pattern. One catches her eye. "Here's *The Way We Were*."

"Gimme a break. That gooey, lovey stuff makes me puke. How about *Texas Chainsaw Massacre*!"

Charlotte pauses dramatically and waits. Stu takes his cue, turning to look at her. Charlotte raises her carefully plucked eyebrows, puckers the corners of her lipsticked lips, and rolls her hazel eyes skyward. Stu figures she doesn't want to see it.

The overhead fluorescent lights buzz softly, creating pockets of bright white and harsh black shadows. The video store is mostly empty this time of night, most people having made their selections hours earlier and now watching them in the comfort of their homes. The few procrastinators, like Stu and Charlotte, wander the empty walkways looking for that diamond in the rough that has somehow been overlooked by earlier expeditions.

At the checkout counter, a teenage girl hovers over a magazine spread of the latest teen idol, her dyed-black hair with blonde roots creating a tent around her head. She unconsciously plays with the silver hoop through her lower lip, looking up occasionally at the wall clock to count the minutes until closing. The regular motion of her jaw and the snapping of her chewing gum create the effect of a metronome ticking off the seconds.

In the corner, a small boy of about ten grasps a game controller tightly in his small hand as he maneuvers a soldier through enemy territory. His body twists and turns with that of the soldier on the screen, recoiling with each gun blast. At every bloody, gurgling, electronic death, the boy utters a quiet stream of obscenities that breaks the silence in the store.

"Well, there's gotta be something we both want to see," Stu says as Charlotte turns the corner into the next aisle. He squats down and bends his tall frame to read the titles on the bottom shelf. He runs his left hand through his long, sandy hair, stopping to massage the base of his neck. His eyes squint and he sighs loudly. His hand falls back into his lap and he crabwalks sideways to the end of the rack.

One of the little black boxes catches Stu's eye. He reaches for it, sliding it out with his middle finger. The box next to it slides out also, and falls from the shelf onto the floor with a startling smack. A dark face of slicked black hair and full moon eyes stares back from the cover. Stu picks it up and gazes into the mesmerizing face, the unblinking eyes, then blinks a few times himself to regain his focus. Putting back his original choice, he grasps the one on the floor. He raises himself up slowly, a few joints cracking here and there as he straightens up. "How about this one?" he asks, walking over to Charlotte, showing the box to her.

She doesn't look at him. "What is it?"

"It's called *Horror Flick*."

"I don't want to see any more gory monster movies. Don't you ever watch anything else?"

He thinks about the question for a very short moment. Not the question she asked, but the bigger question that always seems to lurk in the background. The question about why they continue to see each other. If it's true that opposites attract, he thinks, then they should attract like super glue. Do they? He thinks about it often. But there's always the sex. The feel of her skin. The smell of her neck. The taste of her sweat. That's as good a reason as any, he guesses. For now, at least. Great sex.

He tugs nonchalantly at the elastic of his underwear, and furtively wiggles his leg. "This one looks good," he says, referring to the video in his hand. "It says it's about aliens from outer space who bring the dead back to life who then all go around drinking blood and planning the total destruction of the human race."

"I don't want to see vampires and dead people and blood."

Stu thinks for a moment. "But this is a love story, too. It says so right here." He holds the box under her nose, pointing at it, then quickly pulls it back. He clears his throat dramatically. "The vampires, a guy and a girl, try to find true love and establish a deep, meaningful relationship while slicing people's limbs off and feeding on their flesh."

"Where's it say that?"

"Right here." He again flashes the box at her. She frowns. He leans over her shoulder and nuzzles her ear. "Come on," he whispers teasingly. "How about it?" He pulls back her hair and kisses her cheek. "You know we won't end up watching it anyway." He smiles slyly.

Charlotte shakes her head softly, her long hair swishing gently like a curtain in a soft gale, and lets out a quiet "tsk" of surrender. "Okay. But next time we see a good movie."

Stu straightens up with a big, boyish grin on his face. "Goody," he says as he walks briskly, almost skipping, toward the cash register. Suddenly the tape falls from his hand and he stops, staring at it. His shoulders involuntarily contract. His neck shivers as if from an unseen cold wind.

Charlotte looks at him, puzzled. "What's with you?"

Stu stares at the box on the floor, then looks up at her, slightly dazed. "I don't know," he says. "I was holding it . . . I thought I felt something . . . I thought something moved." He shakes his head to clear it. Shakes out his shoulders. Shuffles his feet. His boyish grin returns. "Scared you, didn't I?" he says mischievously, looking down at her. He picks up the box, gripping it tightly, and continues stiffly toward the cashier. Charlotte shakes her head--her eyes once again dart skyward in disapproval--and lazily follows.

In Stu's apartment, Charlotte waits patiently on a small, old, comfortable couch facing the television set. The faded paisley patterns swarm around her. On the walls, the posters of rock stars and beer babes have, one by one, been replaced with more sophisticated prints of equally unclad nudes and futuristic landscapes. What's the difference, she wonders. Is it the fact that these have frames instead of push pins that make it art?

She leans her head way back, her jet black hair falling, spider-like over the back of the couch. She closes her eyes gently and thinks about timing.

It'll be tomorrow she decides. It was going to be tonight. No movie. No sex. It's all over. Their relationship is a dead end, of course. Two different worlds--he's smart, graduating from college, working for a big company now. But what can a high school dropout say to a college graduate? Where could he take me and be proud, she wonders. Of someone like me who actually preferred the rock posters and beer ads on the walls. But there's still the sex to consider. After the breakup, no more sex. It's got to be a clean break, she thinks. So this time--tonight--that's *really* the last time. I'll tell him. After tonight. After sex.

"Now don't fall asleep on me." Stu enters from the kitchen holding two large glasses of wine, one in each hand, and precariously balancing a filled-over-the-rim bowl of popcorn between his forearms. Charlotte looks up sleepily. Stu puts down the popcorn and wine on the worn coffee table and plops down next to her. He stretches one long arm around her shoulder and gives her a squeeze. "This is gonna be great," he says, picking up the remote control with his free hand. Charlotte nods and smiles unconvincingly. Stu presses a button and the movie begins.

The screen is black except for thin gray scratch marks that dance like severed marionette strings across the screen. The obligatory FBI warning appears. Stu searches under the couch and behind pillows for covert FBI operands waiting to arrest them for inadvertent copyright law infringement. He stretches the neck of Charlotte's top and places his mouth into the opening. "Any FBI agents hiding in there?" he shouts down. Charlotte playfully bats his head away.

"They wouldn't be in there, anyway," she says.

"Yeah. Not enough room."

Charlotte snickers. They turn back to the TV where a shrill horn screams and the words, "Roger Herman, the Master of Fear, presents" appear, then fade away. Blackness. Silence is followed by the loud "Da dum!" of a bass drum as the title, "Horror Flick" appears on the screen in blood-dripping letters. The title remains on the screen for several seconds before rippling like a damp flag in the wind, then fading away. The rest of the credits follow, leaving the screen with the same ripple-fade. The last credit announces "and Reva Trantini as The Man in the Black Cape."

"Hey. Reva Trantini." exclaims Stu. "He's good." Instinctively, Charlotte snuggles closer.

The scene on the television opens with a trash-can-lid/flying-saucer wobbling across an overcast suburban sky. There is a cut to the interior of this drunken space ship, a fluorescent-lit, cardboard-and-plywood room where a middle aged, beer-bellied man in regulation sci-fi silver military dress sits at a small card table. On the wall to his side is a map of the solar system showing the earth inside a heavy red circle with a red slash over it. Next to the map and standing in front of the man is a very tall, very buxom woman in silver leotards, silver breast plate, silver spiked heels with a silver laser gun tucked into her silver pants.

The man addresses the woman in a gravelly

monotone. "Lieutenant Zimba, our mission is to destroy the people of the planet earth so that we may take it over. We need it because our own planet is dying and we must find a new place to live. The planet earth has many natural resources that we need such as water and trees and rocks and food.

"The inhabitants of the planet earth, known as humans, are very stupid creatures. We are much smarter than them. We have a plan that will destroy all humans. We are going to use our anti-death beam to bring the dead back to life. As you know, when someone is brought back from the dead they need to eat living flesh to stay alive. The dead will then begin a feast of live flesh all across the planet. The live humans will try to kill the dead humans, but of course the dead can't be killed because they are already dead. When all of the dead humans have eaten all of the live humans, then the whole planet will have died, and we will be able to live there ourselves."

The man stops for a moment and there is an uncomfortable silence. He continues suddenly. "Now go and execute the plan according to your instructions!" Lieutenant Zimba, who has been standing rock-still and expressionless, nods her head and gives an open hand salute. She turns swiftly and marches out.

"Hey -- pretty good stuff, huh?" says Stu. Charlotte's hand softly strokes the small blonde hairs at the back of his neck. "Are you watching the movie?" he asks, looking at her with his patent-pending mischievous grin.

"Of course," she replies and slides her hand down his jeans leg to his knee. Stu slips his own hand down behind Charlotte's back and leans over to kiss her. With his other hand he rubs her belly softly with his fingertips. He works his hand up, button by button, undoing each as she arches her back and lets out a hot breath, slow and deep. She slides onto her back and he follows her movement, pressing his chest to hers. He reaches behind her to unclasp her bra as she caresses his hips with the palms of her hands.

The two of them writhe and twist on the couch, stripping down to their underwear with practiced spontaneity. On the TV screen, a sinister looking man in a black polyester cape confronts an innocent young woman. His intentions are obviously no good. He approaches her slowly, holding his cape as a shield in front of him, covering all but his eyes. The camera closes in. His pale white face contorts, his eyes wide and white, his lips red, as he looks at her and proclaims with a

strong Eastern European accent, "You . . . are goink . . . to die."
As the young woman returns his gaze, mouth open with
exaggerated fear, he brings up his bony hand and clasps it
firmly around her neck. As he squeezes, the woman's eyes
widen and she emits a shrill scream before falling to the floor,
off camera, presumably dead.

At the sound of the scream, Stu turns his face to the
television set in time to see the woman faint away. The sinister
man in the black cape turns to face him.

"Hey, what's going on?" says Charlotte. "you can't
stop now."

"Sorry," says Stu still looking back at the evil face
that continues to glare at him from the screen. A single bead of
sweat snakes down from the small of his back to the crack of
his butt, like a small beetle running along his skin. He shivers.
"Just got distracted," he adds, and pulls his gaze back to
Charlotte.

"Distracted?" says Charlotte, playfully.
"Distracted?" she repeats. With one hand she gently runs her
fingernails across his cheek. With her other hand . . .

"Mmmm . . . ," says Stu as he laughs, shaking other
thoughts from his head.

On the screen, the man with the black cape, hollow eyes, and blood red lips continues staring. With slow purpose his face contorts once again. His mouth deliberately, painfully forms the words once more, "You . . . are goink . . . to die."

As the man watches the couple on the couch--his face a frozen death mask--a long, thin strip of video tape begins slowly snaking its way out of the VCR's mouth. Silently it slides down the front of the chipped and scratched television set, over the caped man's brow, nose, mouth, chin, to the floor. On the couch, the couple, now completely naked, embrace. Silently the errant magnetic strip squirms and slithers across the carpeted floor, past the miniature landscape of scattered, rumpled clothes, around the legs of the old coffee table, toward the preoccupied couple. At the foot of the couch, the head of the tape stops while the VCR, amid soft mechanical groaning, continues to emit more celluloid, forming it into a snake-like coil. Waiting.

The lovers continue. They pull and push and maneuver, their naked limbs entwined.

The man on the screen watches, his eyes angry, intent. The tape head pulls itself erect like a charmed cobra to mysterious, unheard orchestrations. The couple's movements become slow and rhythmic as low moans and inadvertent utterances escape their open mouths.

The tape springs quickly. It wraps itself lightly around the couple's feet and spirals quickly up their tangled legs toward their waists.

"Hey, what are you doing down there?" asks Stu, "Feels kinda funny."

"It's the same thing I always do," replies Charlotte. "Ow. What are you doing?"

They turn in unison to look down and see the video tape quickly winding around their bodies and toward their chests. Their faces echo each other's bewilderment and panic. They try to get up, but the tape tightens, locking them together. Its climb toward their faces quickens, its smooth surface coiling closely around their sweaty skin. They struggle in vain against this instant cocoon. A few guttural sounds emerge from their throats before the tape wraps tightly around their necks. Like a boa it squeezes. Harder. A crack. Another. Then several more. Two deep breaths simultaneously expel the last bits of air from near empty lungs. The two bodies go limp as the life exits. The face on the screen smiles almost imperceptibly as the picture fades slowly to black.

Chapter 2

Brent Wooden leans far back into his desk chair until the springs and joints creak in protest. His large, muscular body sinks comfortably into the vinyl padding while the air in the cushions escapes with a soft whooshing sound. Lifting his feet, he brings his heavy suede cowboy boots down onto his desk, one after the other, each with a loud, imposing clunk. The boots fit neatly into two worn, chipped spots on the desk where he has aimed his feet in nearly the same precise manner and the same exact spot for the seventeen years that he has owned this piece of furniture. Those are exactly the same seventeen years that he has been a homicide detective at precinct twenty-seven of Los Angeles County, in the city of Los Angeles.

He looks out over his office, a 14 foot by 14 foot room that in and of itself is a sign of authority and respect to the other members of the force. One of the few perks that a police detective can expect after seventeen years of service.

Wooden thrusts a long, thin pinky finger into his left ear and twists it around violently in response to a sudden itch. Pulling the finger out, the long, untrimmed nail is covered in a greenish substance that he examines for a moment, then rolls into a waxy ball which he flicks on to the floor. Or on to a large pile of papers to be more accurate, since the entire floor, with the exception of several very small patches, is entirely covered with papers and boxes of more papers. Even the worn cloth visitor's chair that sits across from his desk is covered with half open boxes of papers. This is done purposely, since visitors are unwelcome in Wooden's office. Which is also fine with most of the police force, who deal with him only when required.

Behind him, on the wall, the clock ticks loudly. It is the only object on these barren white walls, unless you count the patches of peeling paint, the fingerprints, smudges, and the single bullet hole where the previous clock used to hang. And of course the lone Playboy calendar, open to the month of October despite the fact that October came and went three months earlier.

In his left hand, Wooden holds a clipboard containing more of the endless official paperwork. His right hand picks up a pen which he uses to check off a few items and initial a few lines on the forms. He taps the pen against his teeth a few times before putting it down and picking up the cigar stub that smolders in the ashtray on the desk. Next to the ashtray is a picture, the only personal item in this entire room. His eyes linger on the picture for a moment, reading the inscription, "To Brent. Make my day. Clint Eastwood."

Wooden takes the cigar from his lips, taps it against his teeth for a moment while he thinks about this report. Then he takes the stub and presses it against the paper, signing his name. The paper smolders before burning to black charcoal. "Shit!" he exclaims, sticking the stub back into his mouth. Angrily, he crumples up the forms and tosses them in the general direction of where the trash basket should be. It hits a box and falls to the floor among all of the other papers. "Shit," he notes again.

Through the large window across from his chair,

Wooden spots Charlie Baxter walking quickly and officially down the long hallway in this direction. Of course, Baxter always walks quickly and officially using long, stiff strides and with a puckered look on his face. Baxter always appears to Wooden like a victim of an Ex-Lax® OD on his way to find relief.

Baxter opens the door, takes a deep breath, and begins coughing. It's his usual greeting. "Second hand smoke. You're killing us, Wooden!" He takes the manila folder in his hand and begins waving it, simply moving the smoky haze from side to side rather than clearing it. "And you know it's illegal in the building."

"Yeah, yeah," says Wooden, taking a particularly long, drawn out drag on his cigar.

"Screw you," says Baxter as he turns to leave.

"Hey!" Wooden snaps. Baxter turns around. "You got something for me?"

"Oh yeah." Baxter launches the manila folder onto Wooden's desk. It lands with a smack, and the pile of papers in the IN basket slide down into the OUT basket. "Murder case. I'm sure you'll love it."

Wooden smiles without acknowledging the folder or

the insult. Baxter turns again to go, stops, turns back. "And out with that cigar, now! Or I'm reporting it." He swivels and walks out briskly. The door rattles behind him.

Wooden carefully takes the cigar stub between his right thumb and middle finger, and with his index finger flings it against the window in the door, directly at the shrinking image of Baxter. The stub hits with a clink, then drops to the floor, just missing the trash can and landing in another pile of papers.

Wooden runs his large, tobacco stained fingers over the manila envelope, as if to feel its contents. Savoring them. He holds the envelope up to his nose and inhales the scent of a new case. And the scent of smoke. Burning paper. He sniffs again. Then again, squinting. Looking down he sees the small, smoldering fire that his cigar butt has started, small flames licking upward. He quickly grabs the small fire extinguisher he keeps under his desk for just such moments, untwists the top, and blasts the paper fire several times. With a whoosh, a small cloud of carbon dioxide blasts out, smothering the flames. He places the extinguisher back on the floor and leans back in his chair.

"Shit."

Chapter 3

Brent Wooden drives along highway 405, his 1975 Chevy Impala taking up more room than it ought to, it seems, surrounded by the tiny, bright compact cars that swarm and buzz around him. He drives slowly despite the complaints of his fellow travelers. He responds to them only occasionally with a raised middle finger, but he doesn't get angry. It's too nice a day. There's a brand new homicide to check out.

Smoke from his cigar curls upward in front of his eyes before being sucked slowly out the slightly open side window. The morning sun, already hot, dances lightly on his

high, shiny forehead. The music from the radio, classical, is
almost imperceptible against the background of the rushing
automobiles and bleating horns. He scratches at the stubble on
his chin and wonders why the more hair he loses on the top of
his head the faster it grows on the bottom. The wavy mane of
thick blonde hair has darkened and retreated slightly. Gray
shows through here and there. At least his body is fit and trim
even if certain areas are beginning to loosen and wrinkle. Hell,
for forty-five he figures he's doing pretty well. At least he's
doing the best he can. He shrugs and turns off the highway.

He finds the place without much trouble, being just
off the highway. He pulls his car into the parking lot of a large,
nondescript apartment complex in the aesthetic style of a very
large shoebox with occasional hints of Spanish influence. Like
a red tile roof and graffiti in Spanish. He parks in a numbered
stall next to several conspicuous black-and-whites. Stubbing
out his cigar, he pauses for a moment, trying to remember if he
mailed his alimony check the day before. Why this thought hits
him now, he doesn't know, but the image of his ex-wife
suddenly looms large in his mind. Well, if he hasn't mailed, he
thinks, he'll know soon enough. Barbara isn't one to let any of
his failings go unnoticed, or unannounced, or un-ridiculed for

long. He shakes his head violently to erase the image of his ex-wife, like erasing an Etcha-Sketch® drawing. He can't have things like that in his mind if he's going to think clearly about a homicide investigation. But like an old Etcha-Sketch, the image remains, faintly.

Wooden lights up another cigar and steps out of his car, bending his six foot six frame to avoid bumping his head. The door closes with the familiar creak-chunk sound of an older, American made car. He walks toward the apartment, puffing big clouds of smoke deep into his lungs.

At the entrance of the apartment stands a uniformed officer standing at attention and staring forward, expressionless. Wooden recognizes him as one of the newer cops at the station. Very young, very eager, very conscientious, very unlikely to last very long.

"Jim," says Wooden, nodding his head in greeting. "Detective Wooden," says the police officer in reply, nodding, smiling slightly, then resuming his rigid posture. Detective Wooden enters the apartment.

Bob Simmons, a small, broad shouldered man with a thick head of curly, tar black hair and a neatly trimmed beard greets him at the door. Simmons always appears to Wooden like a nervous squirrel, scampering here and there, furtively burying caches of nuts and berries. His voice is painfully high and he talks in rapid bursts. And no matter what, he's just too damn perky.

Simmons is carrying a notebook, overstuffed with papers, forms, pictures, and drawings. He has a pencil officially tucked behind one ear. "Brent," he says through his seemingly perpetual smile. "This is a good one." He waves his hands in the air like a frantic marionette. "A real good one."

Wooden looks slowly and carefully around the room. Tastefully decorated, he thinks, surveying the hanging prints and stopping at the one centerfold still tacked to the far wall. He walks slowly around each room, taking it all in, storing it all for future reference. First the kitchen. A freezer full of TV dinners. A refrigerator filled mostly with beer and condiments. Dirty dishes in the sink. A few noodles, stained with spaghetti sauce, dried onto a corner of the kitchen table.

Next the bedroom. In the corner, a pile of comic books next to a few scattered textbooks on calculus and computer programming. A futon bed on the floor, the wrinkled sheets half on, half off. On the night table, a worn copy of the latest best seller. In the night table, a few odds and ends and a dozen condoms.

Then the bathroom. A mildewy shower curtain. Medicine cabinet with the usual toiletries and medicines. Wooden makes a mental note that the toilet seat is down, and his ex-wife's shrill voice rings once again in his ear. If I'm smart enough to put the seat up before I take a leak, he thinks, don't you have the brains to put it down before you sit? No point arguing with a phantom, he thinks, and he shakes his head once again to clear it.

Finally, the main attraction. He comes back to the living room where he started. He likes to save the crime for last so that he can examine the rest of the scene without bias. He glances quickly at the TV in the corner, the coffee table, some magazines and newspapers on the floor. Finally, he walks over to the couch, a large white, plastic sheet placed over it.

Simmons has been doggedly following Wooden around each room but knows enough to keep quiet. Now the excitement is too great. "Wanna see the bodies? You gotta see this. It's great." Simmons anxiously skitters over to the couch. Without waiting for a reply he flings the sheet off the dead couple like a little boy proudly showing off his new Christmas toy. "What about that? Huh? What a way to go, huh?" he says, suppressing a giggle.

Wooden steps over to the couch, sucking strongly on his cigar, nodding wordlessly. The couple is still entwined, with him still inside her. Rigor mortis has begun setting in, locking them in place. Their limbs have puffed up slightly from a buildup of gas from decaying organs. There is a slight odor-- they've been dead for a couple days now, that much is obvious. They stare at each other, their eyes and mouths dry and wide open with a look of terror and, interestingly enough, surprise.

"But look at the marks. That's the best part. The marks." Wooden bends over to take a look at the marks on the bodies. "There are strangle marks on their necks, but it looks like their bodies were crushed. Like bones were broken. But how could someone do that? I mean physically, how could someone do that? And while they were . . . well . . . while they were doing what they were doing?" Simmons suppresses another giggle.

"Yeah," says Wooden, tossing his cigar out the apartment door and lighting another. "Any clues? Any leads?"

Simmons pulls the pencil from behind his ear and begins tapping nervously at his notebook. "That's strange, too. Nothing. El zippo. No signs of forced entry, nothing taken, not even signs of a struggle for God's sake. No strange

fingerprints. Neighbors didn't hear anything."

Wooden slowly begins pacing around the room.

"Motives?"

"Nope. Not yet. But we're still checking. He's an

engineer. Just out of school. Works for Cobalt Systems just a

few miles away. She's a hair dresser. Works at the Valley

Clear Mall on Henderson Avenue. Been seeing each other for a

few months now. No priors. No criminal connections that we

can find. No big arguments that we know about. Seems they

were both relatively well-liked. I don't know. I just don't

know."

Wooden looks at them on the couch, then at the

television set across from it. Back to them. Back to the TV. He

approaches the television set and bends over to examine it.

"The TV was on when the bodies were found," says

Simmons, noting Wooden's attention. Wooden's eyes move

slowly upward to the VCR on top of the TV. He brings up one

thick finger and carefully presses the eject button. A motor

groans loudly as the door to the VCR opens. Slowly,

deliberately, a tape cartridge is pushed outward. Wooden

grasps it tightly in his hand and plucks it out. He turns it over slowly, taking several long drags on his cigar. He glances at the title, studying it, then squints at some smaller print. Quickly, he turns around, tossing it into the air. It flies through the air, flipping and tumbling. Simmons reaches up quickly and catches it.

" It's overdue." says Wooden.

Chapter 4

Theodopolus Popodopolus guides his '77 Honda

Civic up his inclined driveway, the car groaning and shaking

until its engine just gives up and the wheels slow to a stop.

With one ham-sized hand engulfing the parking brake, he pulls

upward brutally. The car lurches backwards a bit, to be held

precariously as the brake cable lets forth a squeal of tension.

Theodopolus pops open the driver door which drops down and

away, as if attempting to escape from him. He squeezes his

large body through the tiny door, emerging like a blop of

toothpaste from squished tube. He twirls slightly, curses to himself, begins reeling down the driveway but catches his balances after only three small steps. He leans back into the car and grabs a video tape off the passenger seat. Leaning back out of the car he slams the tape cassette up under the potent recess of his underarm, so that it is wedged between the massive flesh of his breast and his upper arm. The tape cartridge groans under the pressure.

Slamming the car door with a metallic crunch that echoes down the block, Theodopolus waddles toward the steps of his home with as much grace as his 357 pound, five foot nine inch frame allows. A dog--a dirty, skinny, pathetic thing-- comes trotting out from the bushes. Theodopolus stops and bends over the full seven inches that marks the limit of his flexibility, and extends a fleshy hand to the dog.

"Here boy, here boy," he mutters with all the sweetness of his deep, gravelly voice. The dog looks at him, puzzled, its ears raised in question. Theodopolus snaps his fingers, or rather rubs them together with a sandpapery chafing noise. "Here boy. Good boy."

The dog, curious, trots closer, sniffing. When the dog is within range, Theodopolus straightens up and lifts one elephantine leg in what is intended to be a powerful kick. The foot's trajectory ends just a quarter inch short of contact with

the dog's stomach, but with the sight of this behemoth lurching

backward, not to mention the odor, the dog yelps and takes off

down the street. Theodopolus shuffles backward three steps

from the force of his own kick, then catches himself and

watches the mutt zipping down the block. He chuckles at his

victory and his own ingenuity as a small stream of spittle

leaves a cobweb trail from his mouth to a small spot on his T-

shirt. "Stupid dog," he mumbles as he continues his journey to

the front door, his jeans and T-shirt working their ways in

opposite directions with each step.

Inside the house, Theodopolus lets out a long, loud

fart to ceremonially mark his arrival. Satisfied, he wobbles to

the kitchen refrigerator and opens the door. The small bulb in

the back spreads an eerie light over an alien terrain of plastic-

wrapped mountains, soup bowl lakes, and sticky rivers. He

reaches both hands in and pulls out a half-eaten chicken in one

and a beer can in the other. With a self-satisfied grin he kicks

the refrigerator door closed, again performing his three step

backward shuffle as he does so.

In the living room, Theodopolus sets his meal on a

card table and walks over to the stack of cardboard boxes that forms the platform for his TV and VCR. Reaching up under his arm, he pulls out the cassette which all this time had remained immersed in his humanity. With defiance he slams the cassette into the VCR. The television comes to life and Theodopolus tramps back to the couch by the card table.

Tearing a large drumstick from the chicken, Theodopolus lowers himself with a plop onto the couch which shoots up a bare metal spring into his buttocks in protest. He ignores it as he waits in anticipation of the show that is beginning.

Once again, the credits waver and fade from the screen. Once again, the trash can lid wobbles across the daytime sky. Once again Lieutenant Zimba, stunning as ever in her contoured silver military uniform, takes orders from her commanding officer. And once again, Reva Trantini's face stares menacingly out of the screen, directly at Theodopolus Popodopolus who belches in fascination.

As Theodopolus watches, the motor in the VCR on the stack of cardboard boxes grinds softly. The cassette tape rises deliberately from the belly of the machine. The eject light begins flashing erratically. The cassette tape pulls back, then launches itself with the velocity of a bullet, directly into

Theodopolus's furrow-browed forehead. The beer in one hand falls to the matted carpet and emits a final gurgle as its bubbling contents dribble out. From the other hand, a chicken leg rolls out onto the huge belly of Theodopolus Popodopolus and off onto the floor leaving a slug trail of grease. And in an uncharacteristically gentle gesture, Theodopolus Popodopolus closes his eyes. Permanently.

Chapter 5

Wooden pulls his car sharply and a little too quickly into the driveway, his tires letting out an annoyingly conspicuous squeal. He gets out, pulling a smoking butt from his mouth, throwing it on the pavement, and stomping it out. He looks at the small Honda parked beside him, dwarfed by his own car. He wipes a circle in the dust and cups his hands onto the window to see inside. The front passenger side seat is missing and the interior is strewn with food wrappers, soda cans, beer bottles, and comic books. None of it is of any significance yet, but he'll get the full report on the house, the car, and the background of this guy tomorrow. For now he just wants to wander around, taking mental snapshots that he can recall later.

He turns the corner and takes in the small, two story house. The white wood siding, the green shutters, the blue steps, the black shingles have all been faded by years of sun and rain to an almost uniform gray. The lines of the house are all off kilter just slightly--no two lines anywhere being perfectly perpendicular, giving a kind of drunken appearance. Between the two second story windows is tacked a smiling Santa Claus, obviously having seen the passing of many Christmases. The slight wind rocks Santa back and forth, scraping against the dry wood siding.

The yard consists of alternating patches of baked dry mud and large, brown, tendrilled weeds nourished by scattered piles of dog droppings. Wooden climbs the three steps to the front door, his boots crushing the brittle Astroturf® covering. Placing his hand on the porch railing, he feels a soft, sticky substance. He rubs his fingers together and sniffs them, then wipes his hand vigorously on his pants. At the door, he makes a hat tipping gesture to the rookie officer standing guard. The officer nods back without expression, and Wooden enters.

Through a short hallway, he arrives at a small living room. Bob Simmons is once again flitting around the room happily.

"Another good one," says Simmons, seeing Wooden enter.

Simmons sees Wooden's eyes fall onto the large, sheet-covered mound in the center of the living room. "That's it," Simmons says gleefully.

"Another couple?" asks Wooden.

"That's a single individual, believe it or not." He waltzes over to the large mound. Wooden lights up another cigar and meets him there.

"This guy's big. Two or three hundred pounds we figure. Not sure what to do with him yet. We haven't figured out how to get him out of here."

Wooden stares at the mound thoughtfully. "Background?"

"He's an assembly line worker at a chocolates packaging factory downtown. Perfect job, huh? 'One for them, one for me, one for them, one for me'" he says, miming a man at a conveyor belt picking up every second bonbon and stuffing it into his mouth. He smacks his lips loudly.

"Any connection . . ."

"With the couple we found a few days ago? Nothing we can figure. Except this." He walks over to the VCR and takes the cassette tape from on top of it. He tosses it to Wooden. Wooden examines it, flipping it over in his hand.

"Same cartridge? Same store?"

"Nope. Different store. I assume it's a different cartridge. I returned the other one." He pauses. "You think there's a connection?"

"Don't know." He scratches his chin for a moment, then runs a hand through his hair. "Can't think of anything. You?"

"You mean like a guy who hates this movie so much he follows people home who rent it and kills them? Like maybe a mad movie critic. How 'bout if we haul in all the critics starting with those two guys on TV. That bald one always seemed a bit wild-eyed to me." Simmons stands there grinning.

"Forget it." Wooden tosses the tape back to Simmons who sets it back down on the VCR. "I guess I should look at the body."

"The baaaaawdy," says Simmons in his best Boris Karloff as he hunches over and limps to the mound. He whips the sheet off with a ceremonial "Ta da!" and stands there proudly like an artist revealing his masterpiece.

"You love your work, don't you Simmons?"

"Doesn't everybody?"

Wooden turns his attention to the huge mass of flesh slumped on the couch. The head seems to be floating on the torso, the man's neck having disappeared long ago between the blubbery shoulders, the corpulent chest, and the multiple chins. Above the man's brow is a very neat, rectangular indentation.

"Cause of death?"

"A blow to the head, obviously. I figure someone stood beside him like this." Simmons stands at the man's side. "Raises like an axe or something." He raises his hands. "And swings it into this guy's skull." He swings his imaginary axe. "Wham!"

"Wouldn't the axe split the skull?"

"The killer used the back of the axe. Or some axe-like object with a rectangular shape. Something blunt."

Wooden leans over closer to inspect the wound. "You find the weapon?"

"No."

Wooden examines the perfectly rectangular

indentation carefully. "So why do you think this guy would let

someone stand in front of him and swing a quote-unquote axe-

like object into his skull?"

"For kicks?"

Wooden turns around to see Simmons wrinkling up

his mouth and shrugging. "I don't know. He was watching the

movie. Maybe he was so absorbed in it he didn't notice this

maniacal axe murderer in front of him. Maybe he noticed but

couldn't get out of the way quick enough. It doesn't look like

this guy could move too fast. Anyway it's your job to figure

out who, what, where, and why. I just take notes."

Wooden looks around the rest of the room for

anything immediately significant. Food, wrappers, and

crumpled papers are scattered around the floor. The card table

set up in front of the victim is still standing. That implies that

there was no struggle, because the flimsy table would be the

first thing to fall. In fact, taking into account the general

disarray of the entire place, everything seems to be where it

ought to be. He tries to picture the crime--a quiet, stealthy axe

murderer sneaks up on an unsuspecting victim, alone watching

TV, and swings the axe into the victims skull without

disturbing a single piece of furniture? "So, what was missing?"

"Nothing. Like the other one. This guy didn't have much, but nothing seems to be disturbed. His money's in his pockets. You can see the TV, VCR, and stereo right here. Even the vast porno collection in the bedroom closet. I checked every issue and every page--not a single one missing. You should have a look at it."

Taking a long, deep draw on his cigar, Wooden lets the smoke swirl and heat his lungs, then exhales slowly. "Okay," he says as he walks slowly toward the door, "let me know if you find anything."

Simmons nods and resumes his gleeful flittering.

Chapter 6

The Turn of The Screw is a dark, smoky, loud place like all good bars should be. Tinny jazz plays on the speakers hidden in the walls. A few bare bulbs are scattered haphazardly along the ceiling, providing a little light, but of course none of them are directly above the pool table in the back. Still, a small crowd can always be found around it, the pool table, watching each player line up and take his shots. None of the players complain about the light. Or, for that matter, the beer soaked table cover, the warped cues, or the chipped balls. None of these things could possibly hinder the quality of pool played here anyway.

Located in an industrial section of Los Angeles, the Screw gets most of its clientele from Johnson Screw and Nail, Inc., the large manufacturing company located down the street. Hugh Dickson, the proprietor of the Screw, had been a machinist at the plant. One day there was an industrial accident involving an electric drill. "Let's just say you should never drill into anything you hold in your lap," is what he would tell his customers if they asked. Not wanting to return to Johnson, and left with a hefty disability benefit, he sunk his "sudden fortune" into opening the Screw.

Brent Wooden had discovered the Screw while he was working on a murder at the plant. The main suspect was an employee of Johnson who hung out here regularly. Staking him out meant many solitary nights in the Screw, and something about it grew comfortable on him. When they case was finished, and the suspect arrested and convicted, Wooden found reasons to come back until, when he ran out of reasons, decided he didn't need a reason. He was a regular.

Now he sits alone at one of the booths lining the far wall. He has settled into a comfortable place on the padded vinyl bench, between a large, gaping hole on his right and a sticky, unidentifiable stain on his left. In front of him stand two empty beer bottles on the table. He fiddles with the label on a third bottle, half full. In a corner of his mouth is a soggy, smoldering cigar butt. Somehow he is able to lift the bottle to his mouth and take a swig from one corner without removing the cigar from the other corner. It's a talent he's proud of.

A few couples are playing pool in the back. It's difficult to tell exactly how many there are as they shift positions in the dim light. Every now and then, the sound of laughter erupts from back there, then dies out. Wooden takes his eyes from the beer bottle to the crowd by the pool table. The bartender catches his eye, as he crosses his field of vision at the bar in the center of the room. He makes his way from one patron to the next, refreshing drinks, wiping down the table, or simply making small talk. You don't work at the Screw for tips.

His gaze stops once again at a woman at the far end of the bar. Her hair is lit from the back, silhouetting her face. She raises a large beer bottle to her face and wraps her full lips around its long neck. Her lips close around its mouth as she tilts it back. Her neck muscles rhythmically tighten and relax, and she pulls the bottle slowly away from her mouth. A small thread of saliva extends between her lips and the rim of the bottle, before finally breaking. Wooden shifts in his seat, crossing and uncrossing his legs several times.

A man walks silently up to Wooden, looking him over for a minute. His long hair is tied tightly into a ponytail behind his head, emphasizing the thinness of his face. His eyes are dark and intense. He forms a gun with the fingers of his right hand and brings it up, pressing it into Wooden's neck. "Bang," he says. Wooden looks up momentarily, then back to his beer. "I thought detectives were always on edge, always, you know, 'one with their surroundings' so that no one can sneak up on them. I just blew you away. It was much too easy." The man smiles and takes the seat across from Wooden. Although he looks young, on closer inspection there are subtle crows feet at the corners of his eyes and a touch of gray at either temple.

"If you had had a real gun," says Wooden, "and were a real killer--I would've known."

"If if if. Right. How would you have known?"

"I don't know. Sixth sense."

"Yeah. You believe in that?"

Wooden shrugs. He watches Terry Juniper call over

a cocktail waitress. Juniper makes small talk. He flirts with her, both of them laughing at each other's silly innuendoes. The waitress shakes her head of Shirley Temple curly hair back and forth as they talk. She goes off to get a beer for Juniper and another for Wooden.

"So, whazzup?" asks Juniper.

"Wanted to see how you're doing."

"For real?"

Wooden shrugs an acknowledgement. The waitress comes back with the beers. Juniper makes some supposedly witty comment that she laughs at before leaving. Turning back to Wooden, he continues, "Well . . . work's good."

Juniper takes a swig of beer, waiting for a reply. He's not surprised. After all the years since they shared a room in college, he knows that Wooden rarely gives replies to anything. Rarely even talks at all. Still there's some bond between the two of them that he can't exactly figure out. There's something about Wooden that he likes. Maybe it's all the interesting cases he works on. Juniper has always had an eerie fascination with death and murder. From a distance. In paperbacks. But from Wooden he gets to hear it first hand, sometimes right as it's unfolding.

But there's something else. There's something about Wooden, some quality, that Juniper actually enjoys. What it is, he couldn't guess since most people find Wooden to be an arrogant son of a bitch. And he does too. Most of the time. But there's something else. He gave up trying to figure it out a long time ago.

"I started a new project," Juniper continues. "It's this virtual reality display. You know what I mean--virtual reality?"

Wooden shrugs. Juniper continues, "It's three dimensional. You put on the goggles--the ones I'm designing-- and you see things in Three-D. As if you're really looking at them." Juniper stops, waiting for some comment or acknowledgement, but Wooden simply looks at him, sipping on his beer.

Juniper continues, "So it's based on the new Septium processor coming out from Intel next quarter. You've heard of that? It's the successor to the Pentium. You know, the Pentium microprocessor?"

Wooden continues to stare in silence. Juniper figures that Wooden doesn't even use a computer. Refuses to use one, probably. For what reason? Who the hell knows? Juniper continues, "Anyway, the principle is that each eye sees a slightly different picture. The way that works is that the computer screen alternates very quickly between two pictures of an object from slightly different angles. In fact, exactly the same different angles that your individual eyes would see them."

Wooden's nostrils flare and his cheeks bulge as he swallows one very large yawn. Juniper doesn't miss it. "So, anyway, it's really cool. Very interesting."

"Three dimensional, huh?" Wooden feigns interest. "What will they think of next?" There is silence for a moment. Wooden takes another swig.

"Okay. So what have you been up to? Any interesting cases?"

Wooden looks at the woman at the bar. A man has joined her and is talking to her. He sighs through his nose, then turns back to Juniper. "A couple murders."

"So tell me."

Wooden goes on to describe the murder scenes in as much detail as he can. He actually likes describing these scenes to Juniper. It helps him organize his thoughts and come up with theories. And Juniper actually listens. Occasionally comes up with an interesting theory of his own. Since Juniper is outside the police force, Wooden never feels any competition--or the need to give him any credit. It works out fine. As Wooden finishes the stories, they finish their beers and order a couple more.

"And nothing to connect the two?" asks Juniper.

"Nothing. Except a video tape."

"Huh?"

"Both victims had rented the same old monster movie. From different stores."

"You checked out the video stores? Nobody strange hanging around? No one follow them home?"

"Not that anyone saw. We talked to the store clerks and any witnesses. No one saw anything."

"It doesn't mean someone didn't follow them home, though, right? Maybe it's just that no one noticed it."

"Yeah, maybe. Still. There's no motive. I can't figure."

There's a long pause. Juniper finally fills it. "Well, it sounds interesting to me. Let me know what you discover."

Wooden turns to look at the woman at the bar again. The man is leaving a tip as they both stand up to leave.

Together.

      "So it sounds cool." Again, Juniper tries to break the uncomfortable silence. "If I figure it out, I'll give you a call."

      Wooden turns back to Juniper. "You think I'm an asshole?"

      "Huh?"

      "Most people think I'm an asshole. You?"

      "Well . . . yeah." Juniper smiles.

      By this time, Wooden's head is beginning to buzz. "I'm a sensitive guy."

      "Yeah?"

      "Fuck yeah."

      "Well, yeah, I know that."

      "So why does she leave with him and not me?" He nods in the direction of the couple now leaving the bar.

      "You know her?"

      "No." Wooden smashes his cigar in the ashtray.

      "Did you talk to her?"

      "No."

      There is silence. Wooden starts up suddenly. "You know how long it's been since I've been laid?" The room is beginning to tilt slightly, like something out of the old Batman

TV series. "Or had a woman cook me breakfast? Or clean my clothes? Or suck my . . ."

"You need a wife. That's what you need." Juniper is feeling the beer a little now, too.

"I had one, remember?"

"I mean a *human* one." Juniper gets up and signals the waitress for the check. "Come on, Woody. You can crash at my place." He helps Wooden out of his seat. Wooden pushes Juniper away, sways back and forth for a moment, and finally regains balance. "Come on," Juniper repeats.

Juniper pays the bill and Wooden follows him out to his car. "Will you make me breakfast?" asks Wooden.

"I'll make you breakfast. I'll clean your clothes. That other stuff--forget it." He eases Wooden into the car, gets in himself, and drives off home.

Chapter 7

The boys of the Theta Delta Phi fraternity call this room "The Study", but it is clear to any visitors that no one has ever gotten any work done here. If the psychedelic wallpaper isn't distracting enough, with its swirling reds and oranges, you have to ignore the constant stare of a life-sized Terminator tacked to one wall and Pamela Lee Anderson tacked to the opposite one. Then there is the smell of stale beer, sometimes faint and sometimes overpowering, but always present. The odor of tobacco and marijuana is permanently embedded in the cloth upholstery of the couches and chairs. And besides, the lighting is bad. Despite this, there is a small bookshelf of dusty classics in one corner. Of course, if anyone had ever attempted to read one, he would discover that entire rows of books are fused together with a glue created from spilled beer, wine, chewing gum, and other substances better left unmentioned.

Not that certain subjects haven't been studied here. Many of the fraternity members have received instructions in such areas as math (splitting a single pizza between thirty hungry boys), science (the flammability of particular gases emitted from the human body), economics (maximizing the number of beers that can be purchased for the minimum amount of dollars), anatomy (no explanation needed), social science (sexual harassment on campus due to studying anatomy on a reluctant participant), and law (see anatomy and social science). Many of the fraternity members have also done close up, detailed studies of the markings on the floor of this room after a particularly successful party. But none of this studying is of the formal, academic type.

The ping pong table has been shoved against the wall next to the small alcove that serves as the bar. A television and VCR have been placed on top of the table. Roger Vermette, president of Theta Delta Phi, paces back and forth in front of the table as the other members wander in and find places on the chairs and couches. He looks at his watch and frowns. The movie was scheduled to begin at eight o'clock PM sharp. It's already eight o'clock, he thinks, and still everyone is talking and fidgeting and people are straggling in and it pisses him off, if the truth be told, because now the whole night's schedule is thrown off and what would these idiots do if he weren't taking care of everything here at the fraternity and it would certainly be nice if they would just try to get with the program once in a while so that things could go as planned. The tips of his ears glow an angry red as they always do when he's angry. He takes a few deep breaths and clears his throat loudly. The others recognize this sign and quiet down.

Roger reminds everyone of a patronizing grade school teacher and they remind him of immature grade school students, so the relationship works pretty well. The frat members have elected Roger president every year, mostly because no one else wants the job. Roger takes it because he knows, with complete certainty, that the fraternity would crumble without the regulation and discipline that he provides. So everyone is happy. Relatively.

Roger clears his throat again. "Okay everyone. Settle

down."

"Yes, ma'am," replies a voice in the crowd. They all snicker.

"Just forget it!" Roger turns to leave. This is a familiar ritual.

Someone shouts out. "Come on, Rog! We love you!"

"Yeah we love you," someone echoes. "Now what's the damn movie?"

Roger, his ears tips once again red, takes a deep breath, and turns back to them. "It's a monster movie. It's called *Horror Flick*."

"Horror Fuck?" The audience laughs and whistles and stomps at this sophisticated play on words.

"Flick! Flick!"

"Where'd you find this?"

"Look. You guys want something better, go get it yourself. I do everything around here. No one else went for a movie so I did it. What do you expect at the last minute? All the good ones are taken and . . ." Roger's eyes get watery.

"*Horror Flick*. Yeah, that's a classic," someone shouts.

"Yeah. Great movie! Put it in, Roger."

"Any sex in this one?" asks a voice, hopefully.

"No sex. Just monsters," answers Roger. The boys groan in unison. "Come on, guys. We've had porno movies for the last five weekends. Don't you get tired of sex every week."

The audience explodes in laughter. A volley of comments follows about the frequency and duration of their personal sexual performance. This is followed by chants of "Put it in, Rog. Put it in, Rog." Rog puts it in--the video in the VCR--and takes his prestigious seat on the front row couch. He sulks only a little.

A line forms at the keg in the alcove, the cheap beer flowing freely. Jared Martin, a linebacker on the football team, holds a beer high and calls out to the back of the room. "White!"

White Album Wakerly sits cross legged in the window sill at the back of the room, hunched over, staring intently at his overgrown toenails. His worn, tie-died T-shirt hangs loosely over his skinny body. He is not a child of the sixties, but a child of the children on the sixties. His parents, hippies who never joined the establishment even after most of their friends did, named him after their favorite Beatles album. At the sound of his name, he looks up and, through nearly closed, bloodshot eyes, he attempts to find who called him.

"White!" shouts Jared again. "Beer? Good stuff!"

White makes the peace sign with his fingers. "Fuckin' ay, dude!" he replies, still unsure who called him.

Jared hands the cup of beer to someone next to him. He can't see who it is, since after years of steroids and weight lifting, he no longer has a neck, making it impossible to turn his head. "Run this over to White," he says to whoever it is, and proceeds to pour himself another one.

The movie starts up. Brad Cohen turns to Dave Renquist on his left. "I could have had a date with Brenda Lebowsky tonight," Brad says. "Know her? Blonde hair. Beautiful voice. She's a sophomore."

"Yeah, Brad." Dave stares ahead at the TV screen as the credits ripple across it. "Watch the movie, Brad."

The trash-can-lid/flying-saucer wobbles across the screen.

"If the movie finishes in two hours, let's say, then I'll still have twelve hours to study for the physics exam tomorrow." Dan Legault is talking to no one in particular. Which is good since no one in particular is listening to him. "So twelve chapters in twelve hours should be okay, right?" He takes a sip of his beer.

Brad turns to Jim Hauser on his right. "Could have had a date with Brenda Lebowsky tonight, you know."

Jim, a pimply faced kid, turns to Brad. "A date? Yeah?"

"Yeah. You know her? She's a sophomore. Great voice. Sweet personality. Nice smile."

Jim stares at him blankly.

"Great legs."

"Great legs?" echoes Jim.

"Yeah. Big tits, too. Tits out to here."

"Big tits?" A bit of spittle forms at the corner of Jim's mouth.

"Yeah. Tits, everything. I told her I had to be with my buds, you know? Tonight's movie night at the frat. With my buds."

"Tits? Cool."

At the sight of Lieutenant Zimba on the screen, the crowd breaks into a chorus of whistles and shouts and various body movements designed to bring attention to their groin areas.

On the screen, Reva Trantini menaces a young

woman, as he always does. At the keg, a small leak develops in the hose and beer begins dribbling out onto the floor. Jared, still by the keg, sees it and picks up the hose. Beer runs down his pants leg. "Shit."

Reva Trantini's face appears large on the screen. "You . . . are goink . . . to die." The face remains. Staring. The boys get restless watching the face. "So, like, what's with this?" shouts one.

"It's stuck," shouts another. Then more join in the shouting.

Roger gets up. "I'll take a look at it," he says, walking to the set. Of course, he thinks, he's the one who has to fix it.

The nozzle pops off the hose of the keg and the hose flings itself out of Jared's hands. It thrashes on the floor, spewing beer. Jared attempts to catch it, but with his lack of neck, he just can't keep it in view. "Guys? Hey guys?"

As Roger gets to the TV, the picture blanks. Suddenly, Lieutenant Zimba appears on the screen.

"Nice tits," someone shouts.

"Thank you," replies Lieutenant Zimba.

"Cool."

Haunting, slow, sensuous music starts in the background. Lieutenant Zimba begins gyrating slowly and slides the zipper on her uniform low enough to reveal a hint of cleavage. The boys begin howling. Lieutenant Zimba leans over, licks her lips, slides her finger in and out of her mouth, then blows a kiss to them.

The beer is now gushing. The floor is covered with about a quarter inch of it. Jared still attempts to catch and subdue the hose-serpent. "Guys? Hey guys?"

Lieutenant Zimba moves her hands up and down her body, stopping to caress her breasts. The boys are jumping in their seats now, whistling and calling out.

"This was rated PG," Roger thinks to himself, staring at the screen.

"I could have had a date, tonight," says Brad, transfixed to the TV.

White Wakerly strains from the back of the room to see what the commotion is about. He stretches his skinny neck forward, but can't see much through the fog. "Fuckin' ay."

"This is for you, Brad," says Lieutenant Zimba, her hands sliding down to the insides of her thighs. "Because you couldn't get a date tonight."

"I . . . But . . . I could have had a date . . ." Brad
continues to stare.

"And for you, Jim. And Dan. And you, Dave. And
especially you, Roger." She turns to Roger and walks her
fingers slowly up to the zipper on her outfit. The boys are
silent. She flings the zipper down and the TV screen goes
suddenly static. The boys, breathing hard, are silent.

"What the fuck?"

After a minute. "Fix it!"

"Roger! Fuckin' fix it, Roger!"

They all begin yelling. Beer is now spraying out the
top of the keg, but Jared's shouts are drowned out. The top
blows and a geyser of beer erupts, thoroughly soaking the boys.
The floor is an inch deep. The boys don't notice, all attention
on the TV. Roger slaps the TV, but the screen is still all static.
The boys yell louder. Some get up and go to the TV. They all
begin slapping, then pounding the TV.

Slapping. Yelling. Pounding. Roger lifts his hand
high above the TV and brings it down with a crash. The TV
shudders and an explosion of electric sparks bursts from all
directions. The beer. The sparks. High voltage. The boys, their

hair standing on end. Their muscles cramped. Electric current zipping through the room. Through each loud, horny, beer soaked boy. The odor of burning flesh. Reva Trantini's face appears, smiling sinisterly on the screen. The sparks die out. The beer keg stops flowing. The boys drop to the floor as a single unit.

White Album Wakerly, sitting high above in his window sill, makes a valiant attempt to open his eyes and record what's going on. "Fuckin' ay, man! Fuckin' ay."

Reva Trantini fades from view.

Chapter 8

Detective Wooden stands in the center of the
fraternity study, scratching his chin. He eyes lock on the
Terminator and he futilely enters into a grim staring match. He
contemplates pulling out his revolver and firing a quick shot
into Schwarzenegger's stoic face. He reaches for his holster.

"Pretty eerie, huh?" remarks Bob Simmons, coming
into the room. Wooden turns to face him, rubbing his ribs near
his holster. "A whole fraternity just wiped out. What do you
think of that?" Bob Simmons shakes his furry head violently.

"Okay. So why'd you call me in? I'm homicide,

remember? I don't cover natural disasters."

"Oh, yeah? How about this?" Simmons hands him the video tape. "This is what they were watching at the time of death. Coincidence?"

Wooden turns over the cassette in his hand, examining it. "Must be."

"You ever heard of this movie before? Before that couple died?"

"No."

"Ever see a poster for it? Hear the soundtrack? Read a review? See it on the Late Late Late Show?"

"No."

"So now it shows up at three murder scenes. Doesn't seem like coincidence to me."

Wooden thinks for a moment, sucking on his cigar. "So what do you think?"

"Don't know. You're the thinker. Like I've said, I just take notes." Simmons walks quickly around the room glancing at each soggy chalk-mark silhouette and shaking his head.

Wooden clamps the cigar butt tightly between his thumb and index finger and squashes it on a table.

"Witnesses?" He lights up another.

"We're questioning the other boys now. They're pretty shook up so it's hard to get answers. There were a few in other parts of the house at the time. All they say is that there was the usual ruckus up here and it all of a sudden got quiet. After fifteen, twenty minutes, one of 'em came up and found them all dead. Except for one kid who it seems was tripping out at the time. Hallucinating on 'shrooms or something. You should hear his story though, it's pretty funny."

"How many dead?"

"Twenty-three."

"And no sign of a struggle?"

"Nope."

"Gas leaks?"

"Nope."

Wooden takes another strained drag on his cigar for inspiration. "Drugs? Were they all doing mushrooms?"

"Don't know," replies Simmons. "The lab's doing a autopsies now. Should have the results tonight. Doesn't look like it, though. Pretty eerie if you ask me."

"Have Forensics call when they know something." He pauses. "And check out the video stores. Get the name of everyone in the city who's rented this film in the last two months."

Simmons nods his head and rapidly scribbles a reminder in his notebook. Wooden walks around the room slowly, observing. He holds up the video cassette and inspects it, turning it slowly in his hand. "So you think your maniacal film critic could do in a room full of frat guys?"

Simmons shrugs, then shivers. "This is a little too weird for me."

"I thought you liked your job."

Simmons shrugs again. "You want me to return it," he asks as he reaches for the cassette.

"That's okay," he says, still not taking his eyes off the video. "I'll return it."

Bob Simmons shrugs once more and scurries away in search of more clues. Detective Wooden continues examining the tape, turning it over and over. Finally he slips it into his coat pocket, and walks slowly out the door, a thin trail of cigar smoke trailing behind him.

Chapter 9

The no smoking sign is exactly at eye level on the door, and Wooden comes face to face with it at the entrance to the video store. He pauses for a minute, then tosses the cigar butt into the trash. It's best to follow other people's rules when you want to get information from them. He steps inside.

The full height, wall-to-wall windows of the store let in the bright daylight, giving it a softer, friendlier appearance during the day. A few people mill around the aisles. The cashier, a teenager whose long black hair shows its blonde roots, chews her gum, impatient, and stares straight ahead at the wall. Wooden approaches her.

"Hi." He attempts a smile, but his mouth resists, the appropriate muscles long since having atrophied.

"HellowelcometoBoxOfficeVideoforyourbestcollecti onofthehot-

newmoviesandyesterday'sclassicshowcanIhelpyou?" She takes a disinterested breath and resumes chewing.

"Well, I'm returning this movie." He hands her the video cassette, wishing his mouth could form a damn smile.

"Didyoulikethemovieyouknowaboutourmoneybacks atisfaction-guarantee?"

"I haven't watched it yet. It was rented to a friend."

She checks the computer. "That will be a dollar thirty five please."

Wooden reaches into his back pocket and takes out his wallet. He opens it, counts out the money and hands it to her. "Can you tell me who rented it last?"

She looks at him for the first time. "I thought you said it was, like, a friend of yours."

"Yeah, well . . ."

"Is that a gun?" The girl has come to life. She points to where his jacket has fallen open to reveal the gun holster.

"Are you, like, a cop, cause if you're not and you're planning to rob this place I don't have any money and there's this lock box with the money in it and I don't have a key."

"I'm a cop."

"Oh," she says with disappointment. She thinks a moment and then perks up again. "So, like, this is some kind of case you're working on?"

"Yeah."

"And the guy who rented the movie last isn't your friend, right?"

"Right."

"He's like a spy or a killer or something, right?"

"Or something. Can you give me his name?"

"Yeah, sure." She fiddles with the computer, making faces. "Roger Vermette."

Wooden recognizes the name of the fraternity president. "Anybody else rent this movie within the last two weeks?" He knows he'll get a full report from Simmons, but figures he should ask anyway.

The girl fiddles with the computer some more. "Stewart Haddington last Monday. That's it. We only got the tape a few weeks ago" She stops for a minute and fingers the metal hoop in her lower lip. "I remember them--him and his wife or girlfriend. They were, like, all over each other. Couldn't wait to get home. Know what I mean? Like, pawing each other in public here." She runs her hands over her face and sides, wriggling and making loud, exaggerated kissing motions for illustration. "Some people."

"Anyone hanging around. Anyone follow them home?"

"I don't know. I didn't see anyone. Yeah, I would've seen someone if someone was there. I'm very observational, you know? I could be a cop, too."

"I'm sure." He didn't mean for it to come out sarcastic, it just did.

The girl looks down and picks at a scab on her finger, pouting. "Thanks for your help," he says. "You may have helped prevent another crime."

"Yeah?" She looks up again.

"I'd like to rent this." He hands her his membership card.

She smiles. "I'll scan it."

She pops open the clear plastic container to run the bar code scanner over it. As her left hand makes contact with the cassette, she pauses and looks directly into Brent Wooden's eyes. Her smile tightens. Her eyes seems to almost glow red for just an instant. "I tink you vill enchoy this moofie," she says, not blinking. She opens her mouth wide and an evil, echoing, guttural laugh emanates. The people in the store stop cold and turn to look at her. The laugh seems to linger in space. The gum falls out of her open mouth and onto the counter.

The girl pauses for a moment, still staring directly at Wooden. Then, she closes the case and hands it and the membership card back to him. She smiles at him, notices the gum on the counter, picks it up, pops it in her mouth and resumes chewing.

Wooden looks at her, unblinking. The people in the store slowly resume what they were doing. He blinks a few times. "I didn't realize before that you have an accent."

"Oh yeah," she replies, disappointed. "I'm originally from Baltimore."

Wooden turns to go.

"Good luck with your case," she calls after him. He turns to see her waving. He nods, turns back, exits the store.

Chapter 10

Beer in one hand, remote control in the other, Brent
Wooden eases back into the thick leather cushions of his
recliner. The room isn't particularly large, it just looks that way
because of the light, airy colors--the blue-gray carpet and the
pastel landscapes in silver frames on bright white walls. The
black leather couch and black leather recliner at one end, and
the black plastic and metal entertainment center at the other
balance each other perfectly. The overhead atrium brings a nice
splash of sunlight into the room, further opening it up. Of
course, this was all Barbara's contribution--his ex-wife. His

contribution is the ash tray overflowing with cigar butts, the spread of a month's worth of newspapers over the plush carpet, the beer cans standing guard around the recliner, and the solitary pair of undershorts that lay rumpled in the far corner.

Wooden presses the play button on the remote control and watches as the TV screen comes to life. Sipping his beer, he watches the movie credits as they jump onto the screen then waver out of existence. Soon the strain of the day catches up with him, and his body's complaints take the form of aching joints and sore muscles. He massages his temples, his neck, his shoulders in a futile attempt at relief. On the screen, Lieutenant Zimba receives her orders, salutes, and marches out. In the recliner, Detective Wooden closes his eyes, releases the now empty beer can from his hand to fall silently onto the Sports Section, and drifts out of consciousness.

Wooden's ex-wife is sitting at a small card table in a fluorescent-lit, cardboard-and-plywood room. She is dressed in a silver colored military uniform. On the wall to her side is a rifle target silhouette of a man with a red circle and slash over his groin. Wooden is in full police uniform, also silver, facing her. His ex-wife addresses him in a monotone: "Lieutenant Zimba, our mission is to destroy the men of the planet earth."

Wooden looks around, confused. He looks at his own uniform, the regulation laser pistol at his side, then at her. "Barbara . . ." he starts quietly.

"Silence!" she shouts back at him, "I have not finished." She resumes her monotone. "Men are very stupid, greedy, selfish creatures. Women are much smarter than men. We have a plan that will destroy all men."

Wooden studies her face. He realizes how long it's been since he's seen her. Her long, red hair sways back and forth and he remembers the poems he wrote for her describing her hair as a cherry soda waterfall. Poetry! Brent Wooden wrote poetry? Even he has trouble believing that. "Barbara. Was it really all that bad?"

"Men are bad. Bad bad bad bad!"

He becomes sad. "We had some good times, didn't we?"

"Men are bad bad bad bad! And stupid. And selfish." Her face softens for a minute. Her eyes relax. She has beautiful brown eyes, Wooden thinks. When she's not angry. He tries to remember her not being angry.

Barbara's tone becomes quieter. "And selfish, Brent. When did we have good times?"

"We had them. I used to write poetry. For you."

"That was *Brent* Wooden. That wasn't *Detective* Wooden. You loved the force more than you loved me."

"I had a career. I loved you and I wanted my career. You wanted all of me. You wanted everything."

"And you gave me nothing. Wasn't there something in between?"

Wooden hesitates. "I loved you."

"You loved your gun, your cigar. You loved your job. And you loved yourself. You didn't love me."

"And you loved every man at health club, the gun club, and the Rotary Club. What did you get from them that you didn't get from me?"

Barbara's face becomes an unemotional mask once again; a frozen caricature. Continuing in a monotone, "The men of earth will be destroyed. Starting with the most corrupt, the most objectionable, the man with no heart--Detective Brent Wooden."

"Barbara! Stop this fucking nonsense right now!"

She stops and looks at him, then continues, "You must destroy Brent Wooden."

"I *am* Brent Wooden!" shouts Wooden.

Barbara freezes, confused. She looks him over and suddenly realizes her mistake. "You . . . you are a man!" she says in disbelief. Her eyes begin to glow red. She stands slowly and raises her laser gun level to his chest. In a thick Eastern European accent she proclaims, "You . . . are goink . . . to die," and squeezes the trigger. Brent Wooden watches, frozen, as though he were watching a movie. His limbs refuse to react. Extremely slowly, like the first peek of sunrise on the horizon, a bright yellow spear emerges from the gun and creeps toward his heart. He looks frantically at his legs, commanding them to run, then begging them to run, but they won't. His heartbeat is slow but deafening as Barbara watches without emotion. Her deadly eyes seem to guide the beam toward its destination. The beam is within inches and Wooden knows that when it makes contact it will fry a black, smoking hole into his chest. He orders his hands to swat the beam away, but they hang limp at his side. He looks at Barbara and sees evil--not hatred, not vengeance--just evil. He opens his mouth to yell.

"Rrrrrrring." Brent Wooden jumps up from the recliner. Awakened, his fingers are still tightly gripping the armrests. The phone rings again. One hand nervously wipes the perspiration from his forehead. He sucks in some air and lets it out very slowly. The phone rings a third time. He pushes himself from the chair, his damp clothes sticking slightly to his skin and to the cushions. The video tape is spewed out on the floor, having unraveled while he slept. From the corner of his eyes he thinks he sees a face peering from the TV screen, but when he turns to look the screen is black. The phone rings once more. He shakes his head to clear it, walks to the kitchen and answers the phone.

"Wooden."

"Simmons. I got the word from Forensics."

"Yeah?" Wooden, shaking, lights up a cigar.

"Electrocution. The autopsy shows they were all electrocuted." Wooden hears Simmons's annoying giggle in the background. "Short circuit in the wall socket, they think. Very high current. They don't know why it didn't trip a circuit breaker. Or blow out anything in the house. But it's all consistent. Just an accident. Not a homicide." He seems disappointed.

Wooden takes another long drag on his cigar and exhales one staccato breath. His heart is still pounding.

"Wooden?"

"Yeah. You find a list of people who rented the

video?"

"Well, yeah. But it doesn't seem to matter. Looks like you were right about coincidence."

"Tell me anyway."

"Well, no one. I could find only three people who've rented it in the last month. And you've met all three. No one else. It's a dead end, right?"

"I guess." Wooden takes the phone away from his ear to hang it up. "Later," he says, but the receiver is already in its cradle. He runs a hand through his hair, the sweat matting it to his forehead. He shuffles into the living room and stops. Something is different. His eyes looks around the area but they can't focus. Going over to the VCR he presses the eject button. The machine's gears grind and the tape pops out, rewound. Looking at it, something bothers him. It doesn't matter, he thinks, as he tosses the video onto the table. He has more important things to worry about, he thinks, wandering off into the bedroom. He has to write that alimony check for one thing.

Chapter 11

Back in his office, Wooden sits with his feet propped up on his desk, a facade of relaxation. A fresh, thick cigar dangles precariously from his lips as thin wisps of smoke lazily thread upward into a cloud which like the pendulum in the famous pit works its way dangerously downward. As this cloud of nicotine and tar weighs heavily in the room, so too do the crimes he has been investigating weigh heavily on his mind. No motives, no weapons, no witnesses, no pattern. Only the movie--a pretty tenuous connection. A maniacal film critic? An out of work actor? A bizarre coincidence? He reaches for the phone and dials.

"Simmons?"

A voice on the other end replies. "Yeah?"

"Wooden. Those video stores where those movies were rented? Place a beat officer at each one. Have 'em report any suspicious characters hanging around. Tell the store managers there's been some shoplifting in the area and we're just keeping an eye out."

"Still looking for a connection?"

"Don't have anything else."

"Okay. Will do."

He hangs up. Still, it doesn't make sense. Who would know who had rented which movie? He dials the phone again.

"Simmons?"

"Yeah."

"Wooden again. Keep an eye on the checkout clerks in these places, too. In fact, get an employee list at both rental stores from the managers and run checks on them."

"You think the clerks have been murdering people? Maybe the cashier's union. They're negotiating for a raise. More sick days or another one dies. Those people even have a union?"

"Just do it." He hangs up again.

Still it doesn't make sense. This is probably a red herring. One last suck on his cigar and he stubs it out and lights another. The pendulum closes in.

There must be some connection to the movie. That's the only common connection and the first lesson of detective school is to find a connection. So what do I know about this movie, he thinks. What do I know about movies? Ask an expert.

He swings his feet down onto the floor and begins fishing around in the wastebasket by his desk. Amidst the dead cigars and coffee grounds he pulls the morning paper. He jerks it open and a few tissue wads fall onto his lap which he absent mindedly whisks onto the floor. Removing the entertainment section he snaps it out to its full wing span, a hand on either side, and brings his fists quickly together. The paper folds accordion style. He swears softly and tries again to unfold the paper. It crumbles into a ball. Putting one leg onto his desk, he presses the fold in the paper onto his knee and with a determination born of years on the police force, slams his hands together in front of him. The top of the paper folds in on itself. In anger he grumbles loudly while swinging his hands outward, tearing the paper in two and launching himself backwards, knees over head, his chair sliding under him.

"Damn it!"

Luckily his office is nearly soundproof amid the day to day rumble and commotion of the police station, and only a few heads turn to see an empty desk with a foot like a flagpole aiming skyward. Brent Wooden lies on the floor, a scrap of newspaper in each tightly held fist. He brings one fist closer to his face and reads the bold type:

MIDNIGHT MOVIES

by Billy Bob Henson

What can I tell you about **Killer Vixens from the Planet Bimbo** that hasn't already been said? I can tell you about the virtuoso performances of its two stars, Bunny Hopper and E. Claire Divine. I can tell you about the camera verite photography or the mise-en-scene editing that stirs the inner soul or about the beautiful story in which two alien sluts' search for the ultimate thrill parallels the moral decay of modern civilization. I can tell you this but I'm sure as hell that's not why you're reading this review. What you want to know is: Billy Bob, just how many heads are severed in this tragic Shakespearean tale? That I'll tell you. Exactly seventy-two. That's right, seventy-two sliced, diced, chopped, ripped, blown-up, smashed, mashed, and simply yanked off heads in all. This sets a new decapitation record in modern films which is why I recommend it so highly! On the Billy Bob Rating Scale, **Killer Vixens from the Planet Bimbo** rates:

Dismemberments:	4 stars
Shootings:	3 stars
Stabbings:	3 stars
Miscellaneous violence:	4 stars
Frontal nudity:	4 stars
Backal nudity:	3 stars
Overall:	DON'T MISS !!!

There's his expert.

Chapter 12

Wooden stands at the door of a large Victorian house

in Beverly Hills, the obligatory cigar dangling loosely. He

examines the house with a careful squint, taking it in for future

reference. It's not what he expected, but it's the address they

gave him at the paper. This white and pale blue three story

house with its graceful wooden beams and angular corners is

not the place he would have imagined to be the residence of the

area's premiere reviewer of blood and guts exploitation films.

He had pictured an inner city apartment above a repertory

movie house. Instead of graffiti covered brick, he finds

whitewashed fences. Instead of litter strewn streets, he finds delicately arranged gardens. Instead of boarded windows he finds chiseled glass. Funny how life can often fail to meet your expectations. He rings the doorbell and hears a delicate chime inside.

After a moment a shadowy image appears in the beveled glass window in the front door and gradually grows larger. The door opens and a thin man appears, dressed smartly in a cardigan sweater, casual wool slacks and black leather shoes. A Rolex watch is wrapped on his wrist, noticeably catching the sun's rays and reflecting them back. "May I help you?" he asks.

"I'm looking for Mister Billy Bob Henson." Wooden holds up the coffee-stained scrap of newspaper containing the film review.

The man draws his attention to the scrap and smiles wryly. "Are you a fan?"

"Um . . . not exactly. I'm a police detective." Wooden reaches into his back pocket and pulls out his wallet, flashing his police badge.

"Oh," the man replies, disappointed. "In that case, I'm William Henson. Would you like to come in?"

"Thanks." Wooden puts the wallet back and crumples the article into a ball, stuffing it into his front pocket. He steps forward, but Mr. William Henson remains immobile.

"No smoking, please." Henson looks at Wooden like a grade school teacher scolding a student. Wooden takes the butt from his mouth and looks around for a place to throw it in these pristine surroundings, but sees Henson's still impatient look. "The toilet's this way." He nods for Wooden to follow and he does so, holding his cigar as if it were suddenly a radioactive nuclear core. Into the toilet, it hisses defiantly before death.

Inside the house, it is as elegant as outside. Clean leather furniture and airy open spaces. Polished hardwood floors and fancy, plush carpets. Vaulted ceilings with crisscrossed wooden beams. And on the walls, the only reassurance that Detective Wooden has indeed found the right man, are expensively framed movie posters from "Citizen Cane", "Gone With The Wind", "Attack of the Fifty Foot Woman", and "Biker Babes From Hell."

"My film poster collection. Very valuable," says Henson in response to Wooden gaze.

Wooden turns back to Henson. "You're not exactly

what I expected. From your columns. I expected maybe a college student or . . ."

"Yes, I know. Most people are surprised. Some, the fans, are disappointed. In public, on television or at conventions, I become the persona . . . Billy Bob Henson." The last part is said in a down home Texas twang. "I started as a college student," looking wistfully at his posters. "I majored in psychology but spent more time in the theaters than in my classes. I wrote reviews for the school paper. The local paper picked them up. I created Billy Bob. It's a gimmick, a business trick to stir up interest. Create a little controversy now and then. I filled a niche. Everyone wants to review Goddard and Scorcese and Bergman and Allen. And everyone has to review Spielberg and Lucas and Reitman and Zemekis. But what about the low budget stuff. The so-called 'exploitation' stuff--a term I should say I abhor. I prefer to call it 'budget cathartic'. It is cathartic, you know. It's a release. Modern life is an unnatural state of tension from deadlines, relationships, crowded societies, global concerns. Man wasn't created to deal with these problems. Man was created, through millions of years of evolution to hunt, grow food, and procreate, and not much more. Then civilization springs up in a mere few thousand years and makes demands that evolution doesn't have time to compensate for. Even so, modern medicine and governments have obliterated the grand principle of 'survival of the fittest' so that any bozo, no matter how incapable of dealing with society's demands, survives. How can these people cope? Evolution gave them the flight or fight instinct but civilization took it away. Can't run--that's not responsible. Can't fight--that's not legal. Can't fornicate--that's dangerous. So they go to the movies where they can run, kill, and fuck to their heart's delight."

"So you think mutilating teenagers and abusing women is good for society? Sounds perverted."

"No," responds Henson with undisguised impatience. "I think it's good in the movies. To prevent it from happening in real life. I didn't make man desire to rape and pillage. Evolution did. Don't blame me. Look officer . . ."

"Detective Wooden"

" . . .Officer Wooden. I'm sure you didn't come here for a lesson in film or psychology, though you could certainly use one."

"No. I came here because unfortunately I need your help."

"The help of a 'pervert'?"

"The help of a film expert. Are you familiar with this?" He takes the video copy of *Horror Flick* out of his coat pocket and hands it to Henson who examines it carefully, his mouth and eyebrows alternately compressing and expanding in concentration.

"Never heard of it. Just a minute." He goes over to a bookshelf and takes a large volume from it and places it on the coffee table. He sits down in front of it, opens it, grabbing large sections of pages and flipping them over. Wooden sits down next to him. Henson finds a page with a list of film titles and drags his finger down it. "It's not here. Where did you find it?" Henson seems anxious.

"At the local video store. What's wrong?"

"This is a film directed by Roger Herman, known as 'The King of the B's'. He's the greatest producer of budget cathartic films ever. The man's a genius. You've heard of *Little House of Terror, The Grabbers, Killer Nymphs from Kalamazoo, Death Takes a Nap*?" Wooden shakes his head at each title. Henson rolls his eyes and sighs. "He's a genius. He created this business. His films are classics."

"So what's the problem."

"So I've never heard of this one. I know every one of his films and I've never heard of this. I checked it in the book, too. It's not mentioned. This could be a collector's item. Or a fake. Why do the police have an interest?"

"There have been some crimes--murders--and this has been found at the scene of each one. We don't know the connection."

"So you suspect me? A perverted film critic?"

"I just need more information about this film. To tell you the truth I don't know what I'm looking for. I just need more information."

"And what's in it for me?"

"I don't suppose I could sell you on how you'd be helping society by putting away some homicidal lunatic."

"No, you couldn't. However, I do see that this film may be a buried treasure that for some reason has only recently been dug up and released. I'm only surprised I hadn't read about it in the trade magazines. In which case, it may be some sort of black market release or a copyright infringement or some other legal scandal. All of which makes interesting reading in my column. That, sir, is what's in it for me."

"So you'll look into it?"

"For my own reasons, yes."

"I only expect you to call me with whatever you find out."

"Of course. Can I keep the tape? I'd like to view the film so I know with what I'm dealing."

"I need it. Check out your local video store."

Henson looks like a hurt little boy. Wooden gets up and walks to the door, Henson opening it to let him out. Outside, Wooden fumbles for a cigar, quickly lighting one and pulling it to his mouth. He breathes in the cancerous fumes as another man might breath in a chest full of refreshing fresh air, and walks slowly away.

Chapter 13

Brent Wooden stands outside another door, this time on the second floor of a city apartment building. He rings the bell. A little knocking around can be heard inside, then the door chain unchaining and the lock unlocking. Terry Juniper answers the door, eyes half closed, long brown hair scattered in all directions. He pulls his robe closed and sniffs. "Woody. Whazzup?" He opens the door.

Brent walks in and looks around. The walls are covered with all kinds of thingamajigs and doodads collected from Juniper's various world travels. Here is an Egyptian ankh;

next to it a Star of David; in the corner, an Indian fertility god. One wall is devoted to a large map of the world marked with red trails. A Japanese mask on a pedestal stares up defiantly at an African mask on the wall while a small, round, Chinese Buddha guards the pile of newspapers on a table. Across from a simple cloth couch is an expensive stereo system with floor to ceiling speakers and enough power to challenge most small amphitheaters let alone this apartment.

Terry Juniper walks into the small adjoining kitchen. "Can I get you an herbal tea?"

"Definitely not. You have coffee?"

"You know I don't stock carcinogens. And don't even think about lighting up in here."

"Don't you ever work? It's almost one o'clock and you're still in you pajamas."

"I was working late last night. I'm more creative at night."

"I can tell." Juniper peeks his head out from the kitchen to see Wooden pointing at a beer can wrapped in women's underwear lying just inside the door of the bedroom.

"That? That's a gift from a dear friend."

"You remember her name?"

"What's in a name. A rose by any other name, etc. etc."

"So you forget your dear friend's name."

"So I forget her name. But her ass. That I'll remember forever. She's an artist. Does this abstract kind of impressionist thing with oils and body fluids on canvas. It's really great. Anyway, what brings you here? Official business or you just want to hear about my sex life?"

"Both. Unfortunately official business takes precedence. There was another murder--a fraternity house all got killed."

"An entire fraternity? Whoa!"

"Well, Forensics says it was an accident, but guess what I found there?"

"The monster movie video tape."

Yup. And I've got it right here." He takes the tape from his jacket pocket and hands it to Juniper.

"Yeah, and?"

"And I want you to examine it. You're an intelligent, well-paid engineer--though you wouldn't know it from the way you live."

"So who are you--my mother? Besides I still don't

know what you want me to do with it."

"Use all your fancy equipment. Analyze it. Look for hidden messages. I don't know."

"Why?"

"Because you're a smart guy and I feel like a fool checking for Satanic messages on a video tape but I've got nothing else."

"You think some Charlie Manson is seeing secret messages in it?"

"Or planting messages. Or I don't know. You come up with some ideas."

Juniper holds the cassette close to his face and examines the plastic container, waiting for some great inspiration. "It's an ordinary VHS tape, I assume."

"I guess. You tell me."

"Can I destroy it if I need to?"

"If you really need to. I'd prefer not."

Juniper pries open the package slightly to look inside. "Shit!" He pulls his finger out and thrusts it into his mouth.

"What?"

"Damn thing bit me."

Wooden looks at him, puzzled.

"I just cut myself on the tape edge." Juniper puts the tape down on the couch; a drop of blood glistens on the surface. He sucks at his finger for a moment while he looks defiantly at the tape. "I'll run it through the machines and the analyzers. I'll tell you if I find any hidden messages. I ever tell you I used to do this with old Beatles albums?"

"You okay?"

"Sure. It's just a cut." Terry sees the concerned look on Wooden's face. "What's the matter with you?"

"It's just these murders. They've got me tense."

"Everything gets you tense. You just relax and let me and my machines solve this whole thing for you. When I've got the answer we'll get together, have some beers, and I'll give you the killer's name and address. Deal?"

"Deal. But isn't beer carcinogenic?"

"So's air these days, but I've got to breathe something. Now get out of here. I've got to get dressed and go to work."

"I don't get to hear about your sexual escapades?"

"Later. You can read about them in my memoirs." Juniper gets up and playfully shoves Wooden toward the door.

"I'll call you soon as I find anything." He closes the door behind Wooden.

Chapter 14

Harry Hufnagle excitedly slaps handfuls of Old Spice onto his freshly shaved face. He rinses his hands in the bathroom sink, dries them hurriedly on a towel. He grabs his pointed chin with long, slender fingers, and yanks it this way and that, examining, checking, and admiring as if it were an inanimate sculpture rather than a piece of his anatomy. The chin is still handsomely chiseled though the skin underneath sags a bit. His lips still form a delicate Cupid's bow though the upper one is not quite as stiff as in his younger days. His eyes, now framed by the imprints of dancing crows, still can pierce women's hearts with their icy blueness. And the hair, now all salt and no pepper, has a close cut fineness with its familiar elegant wave. Even in his baggy, checked pajamas that hide the flesh and muscle inching ever downward on his long, thin frame, he has much of his old charm.

"I'll be up in a minute, sweetums," calls Thelma from the downstairs kitchen. Thelma Hufnagle bustles good-naturedly in the kitchen, awaiting the optimal time to remove her famous chocolate-banana brownies from the oven. Her airy dressing gown flutters in the breeze created by her quick little movements as her fuzzy bunny-slippered feet slide over the tile of the kitchen floor. Sliding to the refrigerator she removes two bottles, one red and one white, and holds them up. "White or red, dear heart?" she calls upward in her tiny, little girl voice that defies her age.

"White or red what?" replies Harry above her. He briskly attends to the bed, flapping the sheets reverentially.

"Wine, silly. How do you expect to lower my defenses without wine?"

"Oh yes. Whichever pleases you."

"Then red for the color of our passions, cupcake." She carefully selects two cherished crystal glasses.

"Yes. Passions." He runs one hand over his slicked silver locks and examines the bed--satin sheets precisely folded and hospital-corner tucked, pillows freshly fluffed and precisely placed, heart covered quilt draped over the end. A single rose in a small vase on one nightstand. A picture of the grand couple on the happiest of their days, the first of wedded bliss, smiling out from the other night stand. And a small television and VCR facing the bed to begin this regularly scheduled romantic interlude with just a bit of old fashioned entertainment before the real excitement begins. Harry smiles at the perfection of it all.

Thelma, meanwhile downstairs, glances anxiously through the oven door in anticipation of her gastronomic prelude to the night's amour. She turns to the cupboard and removes the secret ingredients for the piece de resistance--her aphrodisiac icing for the brownies. She whistles happily and sips from her wine glass, emptying it. She refills it.

Upstairs, Harry places himself gently on the bed so as not to disturb the smoothed sheets, and tries out a number of enticing poses. Hand on his chin, hand on his head, cocked debonairly sideways, legs together and coiled coyly, legs spread enticingly, on his back, on his stomach, head up, head down, arms akimbo, spread eagle, fetal. He finds a perfect

position--arms slightly beckoning, head honorably upward,

legs together but slightly askew for modesty with a touch of

ribaldry. Perfect. "Almost ready, honey lover?"

Thelma stirs her concoction thoroughly, one strong

arm clutching the bowl, the other moving a large wooden

spoon in raucous circles through a white, perfumy goo. "Just a

few minutes, sweet buns," she calls back in reply and stops

momentarily for another sip of wine. She refills her glass and

continues her culinary orbits.

Harry upstairs grows impatient. At his advanced age,

the flame of passion is kindled slowly and extinguishes easily.

Better to save his romantic enthusiasm rather than exhaust it

too soon. He slides out of bed, smoothing the sheets back to

perfection, and turns on the VCR at the foot. His mind takes

him back to his younger days when a couple of dimes would

get you and your girl into a good Lon Chaney thriller where

you could huddle in the darkness, her face buried in your neck,

her breath hot down your back, as the Phantom revealed his

true self, ten times the size of life on the screen. Nowadays all

this blood and guts and body parts with nothing left to the

imagination. The romantic urge gets replaced by an urge to

vomit. What good is that? Better to rent some classic tale of horror on tape and snuggle in the comfort and privacy of your home.

The tape starts with a mechanical growl. Harry sits at the foot of the bed. *Horror Flick* appears on the screen in its blood dripping letters and fades out again. Harry chose this particular film solely because of its star, Reva Trantini. While a generation and a couple of notches behind Lon Chaney, Trantini, like Karloff and Lugosi, could hypnotize with a single glance.

"You're not starting without me are you, snuggle butt bumpkin?" calls Thelma as she spreads her mixture on her brownies.

"No, of course not, sugar wuggums." He'll rewind it before she gets back. He turns to the TV screen as a well endowed Lieutenant Zimba receives her orders. Very nice figure, he thinks, but reminds himself not to expend any energy unnecessarily.

"Almost ready, my little jingle-jangle. I just want to make some popcorn. Can't go to the movies without popcorn." Thelma refills her glass once more.

"Yes, yes," mumbles Harry in the direction of the

stairs though he knows she can't hear him. He remembers a time when Thelma was less interested in food and more interested in the more sensual pleasures. Ah well, he remembers lots of things it's best not to dwell on.

"Lieutenant Zimba, ready for orders, sir."

Harry's head spins around toward the back corner of the room. There, lit seductively by the lone table lamp in the corner, stands Lieutenant Zimba in all her silver, buxom glory.

Chapter 15

Detective Wooden sits at his desk, photographs, records, files, and autopsy reports scattered about. He leans back and massages his forehead in frustration. The phone rings. "Yeah?"

"Officer O'Brady, sir."

"Okay."

"I just left the video store at Third and Harrison. Someone checked out that film. You know, that horror film. It's a little old lady and her husband. Must be in their seventies. Cute little couple, nicely dressed. Real dignified looking, you know. I'm outside their house now. You want me to keep watching?"

"Little old lady? I don't know. See anyone following them?"

"No. Not at all."

"Any other copies of the film at that store?"

"No. This is the only one."

Wooden sighs. "Okay, keep an eye on them. Let me know if it looks even remotely like anyone followed them. Or if anything at all suspicious turns up."

"How long should I keep an eye on them. I mean they could keep it over night or a coupla nights. You know?"

"Just an hour or two. If nothing happens by then give me a call. I'll be here."

"Okay." Officer O'Brady hangs up.

A little old man and a little old lady. Shit. Well, who knows. Maybe they're mad film collectors. Maybe they killed a couple in their twenties, a five hundred pound chocolate packager, and a fraternity full of college students. Who knows? Right now that theory makes as much sense as any of the contenders.

The phone rings again. "Yeah?"

"Wooden? Simmons. I did the checking you asked."

"Yeah?" Wooden's voice rises almost imperceptibly.

"Well, don't get too excited. First, the victims all rented the movies. They made the choice of their own free will, as best we can tell."

Disappointment. "And the store clerks?"

"They're all clean. No record to talk of. One of 'em had a few unpaid speeding tickets. We're talking to him, now. I don't think that qualifies as a murder suspect, though, do you?"

"At this point I'll take any suspect I can."

"So should we hold him?"

"Nah."

"So what next?"

"I guess we just wait."

Chapter 16

Harry's heart pulls into second gear with a screech. "Dear girl, what are you doing here?"

Lieutenant Zimba moves closer. "I'm here for my orders." Her voice is satin, deep blue. "What are my orders, sir?" She reaches up and slides her hands along the contour of her breasts down her stomach and over her hips.

"Dear, dear girl." Harry coughs. "I don't know what you're doing here but you must leave."

"My orders, sir?" She runs her tongue wetly over her lips.

"Orders? I order you to leave." Harry turns his head to the door to hear his wife's happy singing downstairs with the popping corn keeping the beat.

Lieutenant Zimba, with deft, red accented fingers, gently pulls the zipper down the front of her silver uniform from her neck to her crotch. It peels away slowly, revealing first her large, smooth breasts, then her flat, soft stomach, then just a peek of a few curly black hairs rising up from the sexual intersection of her long, lithe legs.

Harry coughs, clears his throat, then coughs again. His head, like a wristwatch spring, flips back and forth between the doorway to the bedroom and Lieutenant Zimba who has now shed her garments and is at his side. His face flush, his heart racing, he tries to look aside, but she takes his head in his and forces it toward her chest. His voice cracks. "Dear dear dear girl . . . My wife is downstairs. We're happily married. Please."

She kisses him wetly on the face as she undoes his checkered pajamas. "I'm here to receive my orders, sir," she repeats as she strips the night clothes off a softly protesting Harry Hufnagle.

Downstairs, Thelma Hufnagle places the popcorn in

a plastic bowl. She undoes the top three buttons on her
nightgown in order to cause a bit of excitement for her staid,
proper Harry. Just more than slightly inebriated from her wine,
she balances the two glasses on the plate with the brownies in
one hand and the bowl of popcorn in the other. "Here I come,
my little joy stick," she calls as she heads precariously up the
stairs.

Harry's head shifts suddenly toward the door.
Lieutenant Zimba's young, healthy, naked body is on top of his
own old, soft, naked body. She writhes mechanically, yet
sensually on top of him, grinding together parts that at his age
shouldn't be ground together. His heart shifts into third and
then fourth gear. His mind is filled with flashing, fleeting
thoughts, none of which have time to reach his mouth before
another thought takes its place. On the television screen, Reva
Trantini's face stares hypnotically at the two of them.

Thelma Hufnagle reaches the top of the stairs. Her
eyes look up to see Harry Hufnagle on the bed. The brownies,
the wine, the popcorn go crashing to the floor. Thelma
Hufnagle screams.

Chapter 17

The phone rings. Detective Wooden jerks awake. The phone rings again. Groggily, "Wooden here."

"O'Brady here." Silence. "Officer O'Brady." More silence. "I was following the old couple who rented that movie."

"Oh, yeah. Something happen?"

"Well, yeah, but, you know, I don't think it's what you were expecting."

"Huh?"

"Well, I was outside their house, nice little place in

Westwood, you know. Just by that, you know, big Chinese restaurant with the green and red lion outside, you know."

"And . . ."

"And I hear a scream from the house and I figure, like, you know, the murderer's there or whatever."

"Okay . . ."

"So I run up the stairs to see what's going on, and I knock on the door. Except the lady's like a little hard of hearing, I think . . ."

"Come on!" Wooden wants to take the next 'you know' or 'like' out of this guys mouth and wrap it around his neck.

"Or maybe she's just scared. So I hear her screaming and I kick in the door, you know, like in the movies. She's like upstairs so I like run upstairs, you know, and I see her in front of the bedroom door, screaming and screaming like there was a murder or something."

"So was there a murder? Get to the fucking point, O'Brady!"

"Well, I don't think so. I mean the paramedics are here now and they say it was natural. Well actually it was a little unnatural if you ask me."

"What? What was unnatural?"

"The way the guy died."

"Which way? Which guy?"

"The old guy. He was lying on the bed, dead. The paramedics say it was, you know, a heart attack."

"So they're sure it's not a murder."

"Yeah, they say they're sure."

"What? You think it was a murder."

"No. It was a heart attack. That's for sure."

"So what was the unnatural part."

O'Brady whispers. "The guy. This like old man? He's gotta be about seventy years old, you know?"

"And . . ."

"And he's lying on the bed stark naked, right?"

"So what's so fucking incredible about a naked old man?"

"Well . . ." O'Brady lowers his voice further. "He's got a hard-on like the Washington Monument."

Silence. "Okay, O'Brady. You let me know if anything interesting turns up. I mean interesting like signs of foul play, okay?"

"Okay, detective." O'Brady hangs up.

"Moron."

Chapter 18

The next day Wooden returns to the pristine suburban home of William "Billy Bob" Henson. He stands at the door and rings the bell, tucking in his shirt in an atypically self-conscious manner. Henson answers.

"Detective Wooden."

"I assumed you wouldn't contact me so I came here to talk to you."

"Detective Wooden, I find it insulting to imply that I wouldn't help out our local law enforcement department. I was just about to call you. Come in." He ushers Wooden inside.

"So you found something?"

"No. I found nothing. I checked the Film Archives. Nothing. I called the UCLA library. Nothing. I talked to other critics, friends, film magazine editors. Nothing, nothing, nothing. As far as I can tell, this film was never made. Are you certain this isn't a hoax. A practical joke?"

"A practical joke where people die?"

"I just mean maybe it's not Herman's film. Maybe this killer is a fan of Herman so he makes his own film and puts Herman's name on it."

"Well, look into it. You're with the newspaper. Investigate it. Aren't you curious about it?"

"You don't seem to understand. I watch films, analyze them, and write about them in language an everyday moron can understand. I'm not an investigative reporter. I'm not Woodward or Bernstein. I majored in psychology not journalism."

"So use your psychology. Find Herman. Talk to him."

"Talking to him is not the problem. Finding him is. He's a hermit. He doesn't give out his address. He's stopped directing and now produces other people's work. He doesn't give talks, doesn't go to festivals, rarely gives interviews. All I know is that he's up north somewhere."

Wooden takes a card from his pocket and tosses it on the table. A name and address is scribbled on the back. "There he is."

Henson's eyes light up. "I hope you don't expect me to be grateful," he says.

"I just expect you to tell me what you find out. I need information immediately."

"More film related deaths?"

"Maybe. I'm not sure. Just tell me what you find out as soon as you find it out."

"I still need to see the film. I don't know how you expect me to interview Roger Herman about a film I've never seen."

"Look, I'm working on getting you a copy. I should have one tomorrow. In the meantime, almost no one has seen this film so I'm sure he won't be surprised, or insulted, if you haven't seen it either."

"Sorry. I have to see the film first."

"Look, I need to find out about this before any more people die. If you can't do it now--and I mean exactly right now--I'll drive up there and talk to him myself." He slams his hand on the table on top of the card with Herman's address and picks it up. "And while I'm up there I'll tell him a psychopathic nut named William Henson likes to masquerade as a film critic and slice the throats of directors he admires. See how many interviews you get with Herman after that."

Henson looks desirously at the card in Wooden's hand held before him. "Okay, I'll do it," he says as he delicately removes the card from Wooden's red-knuckled hand. "Your Dirty Harry isn't bad, but that last part about me being a mad killer really wasn't very intimidating, or believable. Stuff like that only works in the movies. But it was a good try." He points to the door. "And now, Detective Wooden. If you'll leave me I must prepare for a long drive and an interview with a genius."

Wooden's hunched shoulders slacken as he walks to the door. Somehow his victory feels like a defeat. He walks out into the brisk, swirling breeze and, wrapping his jacket tightly around himself, walks back to his car at the side of the road.

Chapter 19

Casablanca is relatively small, with a white tile floor and gray carpeted walls. It's larger than Citizen Cane down the hall, but much smaller than The Wizard of Oz on the second floor. On the blueprints for the R & D center of Trilby Systems, Inc., this room is called Video Laboratory Number 3. To the engineers at Trilby, it's Casablanca.

Terry Juniper walks through Casablanca, adjusting electronic analysis equipment strewn haphazardly on the floors and tables and equipment racks. Ragged loose leaf sheets, taped to the sides are marked with instructions for fine tuning the equipment. In the center of the room is a large audio/video mixer, a dark black table with rows and rows of levers, switches, and buttons. Faded yellow sticky notes, like scattered confetti, mark important switch positions. A tuna sandwich lies squarely in the middle of an unfolded napkin on the mixer. A Coke® can stands next to it. On the right of the mixer is a patchboard of black cables interwoven like tangled fishing line.

The front wall of the lab has a floor-to-ceiling state of the art TV screen sunk into it and massive black speakers on either side. Against the back wall are tall, rigid, grey metal racks holding all sorts of electronic equipment with buttons, knobs, switches, levers, toggles, displays, meters, and tiny screens, all connected in another Medusan tangle of cords and cables.

Juniper pops the cassette into a VCR in one of the racks. He checks some connections, adjusts some knobs, sets some switches. Satisfied, he turns and settles comfortably into the worn vinyl chair at the mixing table. He takes a large bite of the soggy sandwich and washes it down with a swig of warm Coke. His face is toward the giant screen; his back is toward the VCR and the elaborate machinery for testing, modifying, analyzing and interpreting. He pushes a green button which lights up as the VCR behind him hums to life quietly. On the video screen, the credits begin. He turns around to check the machinery.

The equipment is whirring and buzzing and beeping normally. Green glowing lines sweep across red-lit grids. Yellow and orange bars jump upward on phosphorescent screens then fall back slowly leaving firefly streaks. Seemingly three-dimensional meshes hover on CRT displays, rotating, expanding and contracting, like graceful, dancing flowers. On the floor, a computer monitor looks straight up at Juniper from a cramped corner as it flashes numbers and displays quickly changing statistics. Spectral composition, pixel intensities, audio frequency components, frame rates are all being examined, analyzed, correlated, compared, and stored.

Everything seems fairly normal and Juniper turns back to look at the screen as the action begins. He takes a another bite of his sandwich and chews eagerly. The trash can lid wobbles dubiously across the screen. He takes another swig of Coke, then turns to check the instruments behind him again. Everything appears unquestionably normal. The oscilloscope has been set up to display the video signal during the video blanking period. This is the period when the electron beam that draws the picture on the TV screen has reached the bottom of the screen and must take the time to jump back to the top to draw the next frame. It's during this time that extra information can be added to the picture. Captioning, for example, is presented during the blanking period. If there's anything unusual it would probably show up here. So far it's normal. Juniper swallows and swivels back around to the screen.

Lieutenant Zimba receives her orders. Juniper chuckles into his sandwich. Behind him, the oscilloscope flickers abruptly. Slowly, almost imperceptibly, it begins sliding backward until it is tight against a restraining metal bar of the equipment rack. The power cord begins tugging at the instrument case with a short, quick, whipping motion. With each tug, the scope flickers. Several minutes pass as the tugging becomes increasingly furious. Finally, with a quiet snap, the cord pulls free and the oscilloscope monitor flashes a bright surrender then dies a slow, fading amber death. Terry Juniper looks up at the ceiling, thinking that one of the overhead fluorescent lights must be bad. He looks around, then returns his attention to the silver woman and his soggy meal.

The oscilloscope cord falls softly to the tile floor, two live wires like deadly high voltage fangs protruding from the thick plastic sheath. Cobra-like, the black power cable slithers along the floor toward Terry Juniper at the mixer. It weaves in and over other less animate cables strewn about the room.

Lieutenant Zimba receives her orders. Terry Juniper fixates on her missile shaped breasts. The cable makes its way toward his chair. The intercom buzzes.

Terry reaches over and presses a button. "Yeah, what is it?" The cable reaches the foot of the chair, then stops.

"Terry, it's John."

"Yeah, John. What's goin' on?" Reva Trantini melodramatically sucks the blood from his helpless victim. The victim screams, then falls away dead. The power cable begins again, coiling slowly up the leg of Terry Juniper's chair.

"We need the analysis equipment."

"Can't you hold off. It's lunch time." The black cable slides deliberately up the back of the chair, its electronic fangs lightly buzzing. Reva Trantini stares evilly at Terry Juniper.

"Not for us. We got a failing DVE coming in from a customer. They say it's not locking onto the sync pulse. We need to look at it."

"Can't you look at it later?" The cable slithers across the chair back, a hair's width from Juniper's shoulders. The electric buzzing grows louder. Trantini's lips form an imperceptible grin.

"No. It's a big customer. They need it working for tomorrow."

"But you need it right now?" The cable rises up, erect, ready to strike. Trantini's eyes widen.

"Right now!"

The cable strikes. Terry hits the power button. The cable brushes his neck, then suddenly lifeless, falls limply over his arm and the arm of the chair. Feeling a tingle against his arm, Terry turns to look. He jumps up and out of the chair. The cable falls aside with a quiet thud. He punches the intercom button again.

"Hey. Some fucking asshole left a live wire on the mixing table chair!"

"What?"

"There's a fucking live wire on the chair."

"Really?"

"Yeah really. There's a fucking live wire on the fucking chair. We're gonna have a meeting. We're gonna have a fucking meeting right fucking now!"

"Okay, okay. I'll get everyone together."

"You better fuckin' believe it."

He turns off the intercom and stares down at the limp cable. "Fuck."

Chapter 20

"Sit down Mister Henson." Roger Herman is a large, athletic man in his fifties with a boyish cut of fine blonde hair, a lock of which is continually dropping across his brow to be immediately swept up again by a big, powerful hand. William Henson sits at the chair in front of the big man's desk. Herman lowers himself into the large, authoritarian chair behind the desk. The desk is in Herman's office, a rather small room in a large house on a sprawling ranch. Outside, not too far away, horses neigh and whinny. Breezes whoosh through towering trees and rustle the leaves. Still, this rustic atmosphere does little to calm Henson whose normally stoic nature is upset by the occasional kicks of his adrenal glands. He is in the presence of one of his heroes.

"I won't ask how you found me," continues Herman. "I know there are ways, but not many. I like to reward the ingenuity of a persistent fan by giving a few minutes of my time. What can I do for you."

Henson looks around at the office, mostly stark and practical with the exception of the big desk and comfortable chair into which Herman has sunk himself. Lined up around the walls are plain, black metal filing cabinets. Above them, tacked and stapled to the walls, are posters from a half dozen of Herman's films. Tacked and stapled! Doesn't he know what a single tear can do to such a memento whose value is growing yearly?

"This is my office, now," says Herman in response to Henson's silently inquiring glances. "I only produce, not direct, so I can sit in here by my telephone and computer and make deals." He points proudly at the telephone and computer on his desk. Henson continues looking around silently. "Do you want my autograph or something?"

Henson shakes his head.

"You're not a nut are you?"

Henson shakes his head again, this time violently.

"Good. We had a nut in here about three months ago. Some guy, looked normal, like you do. We come in here and he starts peeling off his clothes, dancing around and trying to kiss me on the cheek, all the while singing 'I don't get kicks from champagne'." Herman gets up and starts to flutter his arms and rhythmically sway his huge frame in illustration, then stops and sits down.

Henson clears his throat in an attempt to get his heart rate down. "No . . ." Clears again. "I'm a film critic. I'd like to ask you about your films."

"Ask away. I can only give you about ten minutes."

"Specifically, about a film called *Horror Flick*." He watches Herman's face for a reaction. A smile spreads across it.

"How do you know about that? You must really be a fan."

"I know a little. Can you tell me more about it."

"Well, that was my first movie out of film school. I was a young guy, kind of a maverick. I had gotten a job with Jack Cartridge. You know him--he was famous for cranking out those low budget Westerns in the fifties. So after a few film

shoots, we had piled up a lot of short ends--you know,

unexposed film at the end of a reel. It was still good film and

we were going to sell it to some outfit in L.A. when I said,

'John, why don't you give that film to me and I'll show you

what I can do.' He said okay, so I got together a crew and we

worked on it nights and weekends for about three weeks. We

all put in full days on the regular work, and afterwards we'd

meet at a set and shoot *Horror Flick*. We wrote it as we went

along. Hell, sometimes they'd tear down a set we'd been using

and we'd have to move to another one. If we could put it into

the story, we would. Otherwise we'd just hope no one would

notice that a red Pontiac was suddenly a blue Buick or that

Mars sometimes looked like Ancient Egypt and other times

like turn-of-the-century Brooklyn.

"We had a ball, but when I showed it to Jack he

nearly threw up. It's pretty bad. No it's awful. I'd shown him

what I could do and a week later he fired me."

"Tell me about Reva Trantini. How'd you get a

name actor in such a low budget film?"

"That really wasn't so hard. He was pretty old by

that time and people were starting to want monsters with

rotting flesh that could pull their heads off. Things like that.
They didn't want some old man with shoe polish hair and egg
white eyes who was supposed to scare you by staring at you.
Not that I'm putting the guy down. His earlier stuff was fun.
It's just not scary anymore. People want blood and intestines
and monsters that explode out of peoples' stomachs.

"So anyway, he was real eager to do it and I said,
'What the hell'. I figured having a star in the film, even a dying
has-been, can't hurt." He pauses. "You know he died during
filming, don't you?"

Henson shakes his head. "No."

"Yeah. The cameras were rolling and were shooting
some scene, I forget which, and he just dropped of a heart
attack. We called an ambulance and they took him away but he
was dead already. Anyway, we got someone from the crew, the
gaffer I think, to grease his hair back and run around with a
cape in front of his face for the rest of the film. That didn't help
the quality of the film, either. Then again, it would have stunk
anyway."

Herman leans over as Henson scribbles notes on a
pad.

Herman continues, "Trantini was some character.

After all those years of playing vampires and goblins, he was starting to believe it all. I mean he'd come to the set and talk about ancient Indian burial rituals and Tarot cards and carving up chickens to drink their blood and reincarnation. Nobody wanted to talk to him. Forget about the weather or baseball or what a great set of hooters his costar had. It was death, voodoo, and hocus-pocus and nothing else. To tell you the truth he gave me the creeps."

"Hmmm . . ." Henson takes more notes. "So when did you decide to release it to video."

Herman laughs a bellowing laugh that reverberates among the tinny metal drawers throughout the office. "Video? You've got to be kidding. I don't even show it to my wife and kids. It's embarrassing. That's why I was surprised you knew about it. There's a few copies floating around, but video . . ."

Henson looks up, surprised. "I was told there was a copy on video. I was told by a . . . reliable source, I believe."

"Well your reliable source is wrong. He better be. If I find it's out on video somewhere there's gonna be a big lawsuit."

"You said there are some copies. Could I see one? I'd just like to view it for curiosity's sake."

"You've got a sixteen millimeter projector somewhere?"

"Yeah."

"Okay. But I want it back by next week. Like I said, I don't want this thing getting around too much. And definitely not on video."

Herman gets up and leads Henson through hallways to a small, locked room in the back of the big house. "I keep junk in this room. Mostly sentimental stuff from my younger days."

He fishes around among dusty piles of papers and film canisters, finding two under a pile. He dusts off the labels on them to reveal "Horror Film--reel 1" and "Horror Film--reel 2", and hands them to Henson. "Remember, I'm trusting you with these."

"Is this the original?"

"No. It's a release print. A copy. I made a few. The original is in a vault somewhere at Gigantus Films, the company that Jack Cartridge, and I, was working for. At least I assume it's still there. If not, they burned it years ago. But if I find out someone released it to video without my permission, they're gonna twist and turn on a stake in hell if I have anything to do with it."

Henson clutches the film reels like a child returned to its mother's bosom. He thanks Herman, several times, and departs, smiling.

Chapter 21

William Henson sits in the center of the personal
screening room on the second floor of his house. It is early
evening and outside the sun still shines a phosphorescent
orange of sunset, but the windows to this room are shuttered so
that no light leaks in. The single fluorescent lamp in the ceiling
provides the only illumination--an even, unnatural white glow.
On one side of the room is a large television screen imbedded
in the wall and outlined in imitation wood grain. On either side
are sophisticated, high tech speakers. Underneath is an array of
knobs, buttons and controls for the finest in modern film

viewing and listening pleasure.

On the other wall, however, is simply a white cloth screen unrolled from ceiling to floor. In the center of the room, William Henson sits at a small table, his back to the sophisticated electronic gear, facing the plain white screen. On the table is an old fashioned 16 millimeter film projector, an antique in these days of super-high-resolution-high-fidelity-computer-chip-controlled video. Lovingly, he winds the celluloid through its labyrinthine path, gently snapping the lens into place around it. He clicks the projector on and clicks off the overhead fluorescent light. The light of the projector bulb spills out onto the table, creating bizarre patterns of light and dark. The film threads through the projector with a loud click-clack click-clack sound. A sudden beam of light cuts through the darkness as the credits form on the screen. William Henson gently fingers a glass of fine white wine, takes a sip, and leans back.

As always, the blood-dripping credits appear and fade from the screen. As always, the flying saucer wobbles, hobbles, and bobbles across the countryside. As always, beautiful Lieutenant Zimba stands stiffly before her commanding officer to receive her instructions. Behind him,

Henson hears a noise. A shuffling. He turns to see Lieutenant

Zimba standing stiffly against the wall. Henson stands up

quickly, dropping the wine glass from his hand. The glass

tumbles end over end toward the ground, hitting the leg of the

chair. The wine splatters against his clothes and forms a small

puddle on the floor. The crystal glass shatters, shards and

slivers flying out to the corners of the room.

He looks back toward the screen, but it isn't there. In

fact, the entire room is gone. Instead there are cameras and

lights and light stands and shades and screens and reflectors

and sound recorders and microphones. There are also people.

Well, not exactly people, but green, newt-skinned, clawed,

fanged, horned, cat-eyed people. Some are in T-shirts and

jeans, some are in ties and slacks, some are in skirts and

sweatshirts, some are in dresses. Some have pencils tucked

behind large, pointed green ears. Some hold clipboards in

three-fingered claws. Some hold coffee cups. Some wear

headphones. Some hold boom mikes. Some sit behind cameras,

whirring softly in the silence. All of them are motionless,

looking at him.

Henson turns back to the wall, and Lieutenant Zimba

is looking at him. Waiting for something. Her beer-bellied

commander sits at his small card table desk, also looking directly at Henson. Henson swallows with a large, echoing gulp. A newt-devil with headphones, clipboard, and pencil behind the ear comes up to him and whispers "cut."

"What?"

"Say 'cut'."

Meekly, "Cut." A mild roar fills the sound stage as everyone, newt-devils and humans, resume pacing and running and discussing and arguing. The camera newt-devil checks the shot through the aperture. The boom newt-devil calls "testing testing testing" into the microphone as the sound newt-devil at the side of the set checks levels on the recorder. Another newt-devil scampers in with broom and dustpan and hurriedly cleans up the small glass fragments.

Lieutenant Zimba paces back and forth, repeating lines from the next scene. Her commanding officer sits at his table impatiently tapping his finger. The newt-devil with the headphones, a clipboard, and a pencil behind the ear sidles up next to Henson. "Well?"

Henson repeats, "Well?"

"Was it a keeper? Looked good to me."

"Uhhh . . . yes. Keeper. Yes."

The newt-devil turns to the crowd. "It was a keeper." The crowd celebrates with some low key laughter and back slapping. The newt-devil turns to the actors. "That was a keeper." The commander whispers, "finally" under his breath, gets up from the table and heads toward the refreshment area. Lieutenant Zimba acknowledges the newt-devil with a nod and walks off the set to resume her nervous pacing and rehearsing in a corner. The newt-devil faces Henson again. "We'll start setting up for the next shot." The newt-devil walks away and begins giving orders to the others on the set.

Henson watches as these strange creatures go efficiently about their business. As he watches, he feels the heavy, dark fog in his mind begin to dissipate. These are his helpers. This is *his* film. The wine. The dark screening room. The hectic few days. The visit from that uncouth policeman and talk about murders. He's been tired. He fell asleep watching the movie. He's dreaming. This is his movie. Robert Louis Stevenson had dreams like this. He's read about it. Stevenson would dream his fabulous dark tales, and in his dreams, demon stage hands appeared to help him direct. He would command them to make scene changes, lighting changes, prop changes. He could rearrange, redirect, try out new dialogue, new characters. In his dreams he perfected his stories and when he awoke he would write them down. These newt-devils. The ones in front of him now. These are his own private demons here to help him with his own grand creation. No longer must he ride the crest of another man's wave. No longer must he derive his own influence from the works of others--uneducated, shallow, overpaid directors. Now he can synthesize rather than analyze. This is his opportunity to create his own perfect film. "Wait!"

The crowd stops and silence once again hovers as all heads turn to him in mild surprise. "It . . . It's not a keeper," he says. The crowd sighs in unison and they slowly resume their places.

His newt-devil assistant rushes over to him. "What do you mean? You said it was a keeper."

"I thought about it. It's not good enough."

"But . . ."

"I'm the director."

The newt-devil lowers its head reluctantly. "Okay, everybody, back to your places," it calls out needlessly as everyone is already back to their places. Lieutenant Zimba stands nervously wringing her hands. Her commander sits angrily, hot breath exiting from flared nostrils.

"First," calls Henson, "this lighting is no good. In fact, it's shit. Where's the DP?"

A young looking newt-devil in a T-shirt with a light meter around its neck sidles up, claws in pockets. The Director of Photography.

"It's too flat. I want some mood. I want dark corners. I want puddles of light. You've seen *Alien*?"

The DP newt-devil nods its head.

"I want that! But classy, like *Citizen Kane*. You know?"

The newt-devil nods its head again and goes back to the grips to explain the new lighting. Henson continues. "I want some music, something eerie."

His assistant comes up to him. "Sir. Music is put in during post . . ."

"I don't care! This is my goddamn movie! I'll do it the way I want! I want classical strings. With organ music. Maybe some drums. Something bizarre. Something dark."

The assistant shrugs. "I'll do what I can."

"You'll do what I want if you want to keep your job!"

The assistant nods nervously and runs off. Henson walks up to Zimba. "Okay, doll." He stops for a moment to savor his new found director's lingo. "Okay, doll, I want to know your motivation, here."

Zimba replies in a squeaky Betty Boop voice: "Motivation? I'm just trying to remember my lines."

"Trying to remember your lines? Hell. Who did you sleep with to get this part?"

She leans in and whispers, "Just you."

Henson coughs. "Okay. Your motivation is that you really want to take over this organization. You think your commanding officer here is a bozo. You're tough. You're smart. You're one of the few, the proud. Got it?"

Zimba hesitates. "Okay . . . But do I salute on 'execute' then swivel on 'instructions' or salute and swivel on 'instructions'?"

"Salute. Swivel. Do what's right. Feel it. You're smart, you're rough. You can take this guy if you want. You're in control. And unbutton that blouse a little. I want to see some tit."

Henson turns to the commanding officer who belches, followed by a Cheshire cat grin. Henson points at him.

"And you. You were once the top of your class, a hero. You were on the way up. But you hit the bottle. You're sliding down, holding on to this menial job--conquering earth. You know that Zimba wants your job. She's on the way up and you resent her for it. These living dead she's about to bring to life-- they're you. Metaphorically, that is. You're a shell of your former self. A zombie. Act like it."

Henson's assistant comes in directing two other newt-devils pushing a huge speaker. They place it by the set. The assistant runs over. "I got some music. I don't know if it's right."

"If it's not, we'll trash it and get something else." Henson feels the power rushing through his veins like . . . like blood. He motions for quiet, waving his arms like a conductor. They all obey, unquestioning. The lights turn on or off appropriately, bathing the set in gloomy pools of light and shadow and dark, evil corners. A mist invades the set and flows ominously throughout in pockets of swirling obscurity. Henson nods, approvingly. "Sound," he calls out. The music begins, a haunting piece of shrill violins that threads through the marrow of his skeleton and weaves up the spinal column. He smiles even as he shivers. Yes, this is good. "Sound," he calls out.

"Camera." The camera begins whirring softly. A voice replies "Rolling." "Action," he calls.

Lieutenant Zimba walks in. Her commanding officer gives her orders for the destruction of the people of earth. She listens obediently, then salutes, swivels, and turns to exit.

"Cut," yells Henson. "That was good, but something's still missing." The camera continues its quiet whir. The mist remains thick, hovering and surging. The haunting music continues snaking its way through his eyes and ears and fingertips and into his brain. Lieutenant Zimba and the commanding officer remain motionless like mannequins, their eyes cutting him with sharp glances.

"I said 'cut'! What's going on here! This is my movie! When I say 'cut' . . ." He turns around and in the black velvet blackness he can see only hundreds of pairs of red cat eyes glowing at him. A spotlight clicks on, aimed somewhere behind the pairs of cat eyes. It approaches him slowly and directly, the cat eyes parting for it.

"I said 'cut'," he repeats, but it is weaker than before. The spotlight approaches and within it is a dark object, wrapped in the mist, which reflects the light like dewy cobwebs. It is difficult to make out the object until it is about a foot in front of him. He feels the hairs rise on the back of his neck. A drop of sweat forces itself from a pore at his temple to plunge down his cheek and hold on precariously at the bottom of his chin. The object in the spotlight is a man in a cape so black it appears to be the emptiness of space itself. It opens up suddenly.

"Mister Trantini," says Henson, now more like a little boy than a masterful director. "I said 'cut', but nobody listened. It's my movie."

Trantini's eyes flash within his waxen face. He says the words slowly. "It is not your moofie. It is my life." With that, smoke begins rising from the floor, burned by the intense heat of the spotlight. Then flames, bright yellow and orange, shoot upward like gas jets, engulfing Trantini so that only his white face and glaring eyes are visible within. Henson trips backwards as a flame sears the tip of his nose. He falls onto the floor. Behind the flame, the red cat eyes continue to silently stare at him. He scrambles crab-like on the floor. The flame spreads, becoming a wall with Trantini's face like a mask hung upon it. He jumps up, his feet treadmilling to get a grip on the smooth tile floor, and spins around, face to face with Zimba. He puts a hand on her arm and as he does so, she too bursts into flame, melting into a sticky puddle on the floor. Henson pulls his hand back, burnt and covered in a dripping, gooey substance that was once Zimba. The commanding officer then also bursts into flames. The flames from Trantini, Zimba, and the commanding officer quickly join into a wall, completely surrounding him and closing in. The heat is intense and Henson can feel his clothes beginning to burn. His fingertips turn black. His hair begins to curl. He smells the odor of burning hair and clothes and flesh as the wall of fire closes in. He opens his mouth, screaming wildly, but no sound emerges.

Chapter 22

Brent Wooden takes one long, last, savory draw on his cigar before tossing it on the ground, stamping it out, and sweeping it into a bed of flowers. He looks at Henson's house as he stands at the front door and a shiver runs through his spine. He doesn't like the character. There's something about him. His intellectual snobbery and patronizing demeanor. The pristine perfection of the house. The man's dress; the man's voice. The smoothness seems to hide something, like the polished red skin of an apple can hide a worm-devoured interior. Maybe it's something else. Maybe it's not even

Henson, but just this case which has been eating at him--the
lack of clues, evidence, motivation. And progress. In the past
few days he's made absolutely no progress. The murders have
been continuing and he has entirely no possibilities, no links
but for a low budget B movie that is beginning to look more
and more like a dead end.

Henson breaths in and rings the doorbell. No answer.
Come on, are you taking a shit? He smiles at the thought of
Henson doing something so vulgar. Definitely Henson's an
ironic contrast to the persona he's created for the newspapers.

He rings again. No answer. Wooden knocks loudly.
"Henson, where the hell are you?" he shouts. He looks around
but doesn't see anything. He walks around back and smells the
faint aroma of a backyard barbecue somewhere nearby. He
steps onto the manicured lawn and watches, with some little
pleasure, as the fine blades are matted and crushed beneath his
feet. Around the side of the house--no Henson. Around the
back of the house to the gently sloping yard of plush grass and
majestic trees, perfectly planned. Does someone live here,
thinks Wooden? It looks like no human being has ever set foot
here, other than the gardener with his mower and clippers. So
what good is it? If you can't run around on it. Or shoot some

hoops. That's what he'd do--build a basketball court--if this place was his. And a pool. And a big shed for storing things. Manly things--you know--like power tools. This guy's probably never even picked up a power tool. Doesn't know where the on/off switch is.

He pauses. Well, he thinks, I guess this does make a pretty picture from the upper floors, though. He turns to look upward at the house. On the second floor, with the window shades closed, the sun casts strange, dancing reflections on the windows. He pauses for a moment, looking at the reflections on the window, suddenly realizing that those are not reflections. Those are flames. Behind the shades. Inside the room. A fire! The house is burning!

Wooden runs back around to the front door. The door is locked. He thinks for a moment about all those movies where the policeman shoots off the lock. Right. Try that and you're lucky if the bullet doesn't ricochet back into your chest. Or jam the lock for good. Or kill some person who happens to be behind the door. Instead, he takes a large white rock from the rock garden out front and with a few heavy blows, smashes the small rectangular window on the door. He calls into the house: "Henson!" There's no reply.

He takes off his shirt and wraps it around his hand. Reaching in the window he feels for the bolt lock. Unfortunately, this bolt lock requires a key from the inside-- great for security, lousy for emergencies. Picking up his rock once more, he heaves it at a ground floor window, shattering it to small, disorganized, ugly pieces. Had he time to stop and think about it, Wooden would have to admit that the destruction of this house is giving him some dark pleasure. He clears the glass from the frame using his shirt-swathed arm, and climbs in.

"Henson!" he yells, bounding up the stairs. Smoke is seeping out of the bottom of the door of one of the rooms. Wrapping his hand in his shirt, he grasps the doorknob, turns it, and throws it open, jumping out of the way of the built up cloud of smoke and heat that exits. He looks in. In the center of the room, Henson is slumped over by a small table, a glass of wine on the floor. A small film projector is jammed, film radiating from it like snakes from Medusa's head. On a projection screen on the far wall, a face glowers at Henson from the film frame stuck in the projector. It is Reva Trantini with his notorious, evil, hypnotizing stare. Wooden rushes in, his hand covering his mouth. It looked, for an instant, as though Trantini's face turned toward him as he burst into the room. Surely it was his imagination.

Sparks fly from the jammed projector, feeding the fire that is climbing the walls of the room. He rushes to Henson and shakes him.

"Henson!" he yells again into Henson's ear. "Henson!" Henson remains lifeless, but Wooden leans over and feels Henson's quick breath on his face. He seems to be in a trance, or perhaps drugged from something in the wine. Suddenly, a shower of hot sparks rains down on him from the projector. He backs away toward a wall where a tongue of flame reaches out and licks his shoulders. He spins around, then back to Henson at the table. He reaches for Henson when one of the film strips leaps out from the projector and wraps itself around his hand! It actually leapt out like an animal! It fucking leapt out! Wooden stares in shock at the film coiling itself tightly around his wrist. He reaches over to grab it with his left hand when another strip leaps out and wraps itself around both hands. He yanks his hand backward, pulling the projector off the table onto the floor. Now another strip wraps around his legs and squeezes them together. Losing his balance Wooden topples onto the floor as the celluloid serpents slither over him, constricting his limbs. The flames on the walls crowd

toward him. Henson remains slumped and oblivious in his

chair. "Henson!" Wooden yells at the top of his lungs to still no

reply. A dark wisp of smoke enters Wooden's lungs, scratching

at its walls and evoking deep coughing spasms.

This is just film, Wooden thinks, looking down at

his celluloid handcuffs. It's just film. He draws his hands up to

his mouth and bites it, pulling away with his hands as hard as

he can. It wriggles in his mouth like something alive, but after

a moment it breaks. His hands fly outward. In his mouth, the

wriggling film strip brushes his tongue and he spits it out in

disgust. He reaches down toward his feet and twists the film.

Another strip shoots out from the projector and wraps around

his hand. All of the strips squeeze the blood from his limbs. His

left foot has already gone numb. Curling his wrist, he clenches

the strip which is attached to it. The other end of the strip is

still attached to the projector. Pulling fiercely he swings the

projector above his head. The film breaks and the projector

smashes against the wall, landing in a pile at the floor. Wooden

looks up and Trantini's face is still staring at him. He blinks;

the face is gone.

The film is still tightening around his wrists and

ankles. The smoke above him lowers oppressively. Reaching up, he pulls Henson's body out of its chair and places his arms under Henson's. Like a life guard rescuing a drowning swimmer, Wooden slides across the floor propelled unevenly by his one good leg. The smoke and hot air still burn at his lungs. The flames taunt him from the walls, taking swats at him and seemingly laughing like fraternity boys paddling a new pledge. He slides out the door of the room. One large yellow-red burst flails at him outside the room, setting the wall above the doorway aflame.

As he exits the room, he feels the film strips loosen just slightly. He manages to get up on his right leg, lifting Henson with him. Henson stirs, but is still not conscious. He drags Henson down the stairs. The film strips loosen and drop off. Feeling begins to return to his leg and wrists. Still, great flames shoot through the house, up the walls, down the staircases with savagery. Wooden drags Henson, now coughing and twitching, to the broken window on the ground floor. Wooden climbs out then reaches in and pulls Henson out. A serpent tongue of flame blasts out after them, igniting Henson's clothes, then retreating back into the house. Wooden throws Henson to the ground and pats out the clothing fire. Henson coughs violently, spitting charcoal phlegm onto the walk. He opens his eyes, looks up at the house. He looks deeply into Wooden's soot-covered face. "You broke my window," he scolds, then falls back, unconscious.

Chapter 23

Brent Wooden leans back on his police car and inhales deeply of a soothing cigar while he watches William Henson's house burn. The fire fighters are there, doing their best, but it's out of control. At this point, they are concerned only with containing it from spreading, but there seems to be no hope for the house.

He watches and thinks about what went on inside. Living flames; leaping and undulating film strips; a glowering, frightful face. Did it occur? What exactly is going on? Henson remembers only starting the film in the projector. Then he fell asleep and had some bizarre nightmare that he can't remember fully. He remembers nothing else--no flames, film, or faces.

Wooden rubs his left foot which still aches desperately. Then he takes his palms and presses them against his face and rubs them upward through his thinning hair. The flames of the house roar, and in their swirling and writhing, there emerges a hypnotizing face staring threateningly, and directly, at him. He blinks. It is gone.

Chapter 24

Police Chief Sorrington is a small, skinny man with fine, red hair parted on the side and swept parabolically across his forehead. He has a pale, freckle-faced little head and small, little boy fingers. He dresses in conservative, three piece suits in order to look more like his true age, which is forty-three, but instead he looks more like a high school boy whose mom dressed him up nice for school pictures.

His office holds an impressive collection of books and magazines on law, criminology, psychology, and many other subjects. Sorrington has even read a few of them. They are placed strategically around the room for effect. In a case against the side wall, trophies are displayed, many of them bought for a good price at garage sales and flea markets. Behind him is a framed diploma above a framed picture of him shaking the hand of President Reagan. The diploma is real. The other picture is real also--it's just the president that is a cardboard cutout. Even the papers spread out on his desk and the half-full coffee cup are carefully arranged before visitors enter to give exactly the right impression.

Sorrington leans back behind his massive mahogany desk which is the symbol of his authority, until just his head is visible to Wooden sitting on the opposite side. To Wooden, Sorrington appears like a disembodied head placed squarely on the desk.

"So what's going on?" asks the head with its little boy voice. "I was told you pulled some guy out of a burning house. Is there some connection with the cases you've been working on?"

"There's some connection, but I'm not sure what." Wooden longs for a smoke but it's not allowed in the police chief's office. Instead he nervously twirls an imaginary cigar between his fingers. The head looks at him, wanting more information. Wooden twirls some more and looks distractedly away.

The head continues. "So these are definitely homicides?"

"Homicide? I don't know. What's the definition of 'homicide'?"

The head screws up its little mouth in a peevish manner. "What's the definition of 'homicide'? You're a detective, you better well know that definition!"

"It's intent to kill, right? The legal definition."

"Yeah, that's part of it . . ."

"Well, there's intent all right."

"So you have a suspect."

"Kind of."

"What do you mean, kind of?" Wooden doesn't answer but still twirls his imaginary cigar and continues to look away. The head tries to coax more information, "Is there a connection to those videos you've found?"

"Yes."

"So what is it? Do I have to guess?"

Wooden remains silent. The head takes a few slow, deep breaths. "Okay, Wooden, there's something strange going on here. Maybe today's heroics have upset you a little. That's okay. Take some time off. Unwind. I can put someone else on the case. Maybe . . ."

Wooden looks at the head and it pauses. Wooden leans forward. "There's something strange about this case."

The head stops, curious. "Okay."

"Something weird happened in that house."

"Weird like what?"

"Weird like . . . like . . ." Wooden pauses, hesitates. He leans closer. "What do you feel about uhhh . . . psychic stuff."

"Psychic stuff? Like knowing what my wife is making for dinner tonight without asking?"

"Well, kind of . . . "

"Like dreaming about my Uncle's death the night before it actually happened?"

"Yeah, yeah. That kind of thing."

"You mean like that guy on TV who bends cooking utensils with his brain?"

"Yeah, exactly. See . . ."

"You mean like little green men from other planets who abscond with earth woman for their own perverse pleasures."

"Well, not exactly that, but . . ."

"You mean like ghosts and goblins and bogeymen wrapped in bandages who suck blood and hide under the beds of little kids?"

The two men pause, looking at each other. "Because if I thought that's what you mean," continues the head, "I'd let you go on the spot. I'd kick your ass right out of this office, this building! We've got enough problems dealing with crazies killing people out there, we don't need crazies in here, too. So if you're gonna tell me that this is some alien plot to take over earth, I'd suggest you keep it to yourself, understand?"

For a brief, uncomfortable moment, the two of them look at each other. Then the head relaxes; the red drains from its face. "So what about this movie that keeps showing up. You have it analyzed?"

Wooden leans back slowly and brings his invisible cigar to his mouth and bites on it. "Yeah. That guy in the fire talked to the director to get info about it. I talked to him, but I didn't get anything useful out of it. I also gave it to an engineer friend . . ." Wooden freezes and his breathing picks up speed. "Shit!"

"What?"

"I . . . I've got to go."

"We're not done."

"I . . . I have to go to the bathroom." The head looks at him. Wooden squeezes his legs together and grimaces. "Real bad." Before the head can say anything, Wooden darts out of the office, pushing and squeezing past people, down the stairs and into his office. He picks up the phone and dials. A voice answers.

"Terry Juniper," says Wooden.

"Just a minute, I'll see if he's in," responds the voice at the other end. There is a pause, frighteningly long. Wooden hears his own heartbeat as if pumped directly into the mouthpiece and amplified by the earpiece into his ear. Seconds tick away like minutes. Finally, a click.

"Terry here." Wooden breaths a heavy sigh. Terry jokes, "Is this an obscene phone call?"

"Terry, this is Brent. Have you analyzed the video?"

"Woody, sorry, I meant to, but I've . . ."

"Don't!"

A pause. "Why?"

"There's something about it. I need to talk to you.

Just don't touch it."

"Well, I've got it in the player right now. In fact . . ."

"Pull it out! Now!"

"Brent, I . . ."

"Now!"

There is a pause. "Slow down. Let me just tell you. I started analyzing it and some interesting stuff started showing."

"What? What stuff?"

"Well, everything was okay for the first, I don't know, ten minutes. Then the equipment started doing some weird things."

"Like what?"

"Well, just giving strange readings. I don't know. It just started. I need to look at it some more. That's why I . . ."

"Look, whatever you found can wait. It's dangerous."

"A movie is dangerous?"

"Just wait 'til I get there, okay? Just wait. I'll be there in twenty minutes. In the meantime take the tape out of the player and put it away. Better yet, lock it up."

"Brent, what's it gonna do, eat me?"

"Just do it! I'll talk to you when I get there."

"Brent . . ."

"Don't argue." Softer, "As a friend, do it. Please."

"Okay, okay. I'll wait for you. Twenty minutes,
right?"

"I'm leaving now."

Chapter 25

Terry Juniper hangs up. He looks up at Reva Trantini staring back from the screen in front of him. An involuntary shiver attacks his neck. He reaches behind him to turn off the VCR, but the readings on the electronic equipment catch his attention once again. He scratches his head. Weird, he thinks, and instead of hitting the STOP button, he hits REWIND instead.

This is just strange, he thinks to himself. On the screen there is an almost unmoving view of this vampire guy staring straight out. Yet the equipment is jumping and beeping

like there's lots of activity. Yet there's only this face staring
back.

Juniper backs up to the scene where Trantini is
drinking the blood of his victim. Pretty hokey, he thinks.
Everything seems normal--the frequency characteristics, the
spectral densities, the synchronization pulses. The amber
Lissajous pattern on the oscilloscope screen turns slowly like
the outline of a rotating rose blossom. The red bars of the audio
frequency analyzer bounce happily up and down. Then on the
screen, Trantini looks forward, seemingly at Juniper himself,
and announces in his thick Eastern European accent, "You . . .
are goink . . . to die." As Trantini stares, the graceful flower
slowly wilts on the oscilloscope display screen, becoming a
random childish scrawl. The bar graphs begin jumping
erratically. The computer on the floor staring up at him records
glitches and extraneous signals as numbers dance on its screen.
But nothing is happening! Nothing is changing on the video!
There is only a picture of a man staring outward. There isn't
even any sound. It doesn't make sense.

Juniper starts thinking, analyzing. This is an
engineering problem to solve. He begins pacing and talking to
himself. "It looks like there's nothing going on but the

equipment says there is. So what's going on? Something that I just can't see, right? Okay. What is it? Something on occasional frames that go by too quickly for me to catch. A subliminal message, maybe. That might be exactly what Brent's looking for."

Juniper hits the *PAUSE* button and looks at the stopped frame on the screen. It is a single frame of Reva Trantini staring back. Using the large round knob on the control panel in front of him, he advances the video, frame by frame. Still only Reva Trantini stares back at him. No hidden pictures. No subliminal messages. Only Trantini. He turns back to the equipment. The scribbles are zigzagging erratically across the display. The bars are jumping. The computer is still pouring out numbers and statistics.

"This is impossible!" he announces to himself. "The tape is paused! It's not even playing and I'm getting crazy data." Terry Juniper stands up and begins pacing. "Okay, this can't be. So I'm making a wrong assumption. Like what? Like maybe the equipment isn't connected to the VCR. Maybe I'm connected to some other input. I must have something hooked up wrong." He carefully traces the connections amid the tangle of cables and connectors under the malevolent gaze of Reva

Trantini. The cables are connected correctly.

"Noise. Maybe. From what? From the building's power system. Is the building's power coupling into the equipment? It's possible but I wouldn't get these readings unless there was sure some big problem with the power system. Some really big problem. It can't be that. Okay, what else? What else?"

Terry Juniper can't think of anything else so he presses PLAY and continues pacing as he watches his electronic displays and Reva Trantini watches him. And as he watches, and the displays keep flashing and glowing and beeping and buzzing, Juniper doesn't notice that the wires and cables are also buzzing. He doesn't notice the increasing humming of the wall sockets and light switches. He doesn't notice the intensifying glow from Trantini's evil eyes. He notices only the numbers being spit out faster, the bars jumping higher, quicker, and more erratically, and the childish scribble slashing across the display faster and faster until it reaches a terrifying pace. As he leans closer, the little display explodes, sending glass and sparks flying outward into his leg. He jumps backward. His leg is cut from the glass, but he doesn't notice as all of the cables are now twitching spasmodically. All of the equipment is jumping and rattling. For a long moment he stares at the cables, buzzing and jerking, and the equipment, hopping and clattering. Something weird's going on, he thinks.

He reaches for the power switch of the VCR, but as he touches it, he gets an unpleasant shock and pulls his hand back. He looks at it for a moment, bewildered. None of this makes sense. He spins around to locate the main power switch on the control table but is frozen momentarily by the glare of Reva Trantini on the screen. As he reaches for the power switch, sparks begin shooting out from it and he pulls back his hand, redirecting it for the intercom button. He presses it, and it too shocks him. He pulls his hand away and into his mouth. He looks around. All the cables are dancing and buzzing and the electronic equipment is sparking while Reva Trantini looks on in delight at this frantic ritual. Terry Juniper shudders. He sees the laboratory exit, and the gyrating cables and sputtering equipment between him and it. Here goes, he thinks, and dashes for the door.

Chapter 26

Wooden is in his car, puffing heavily on a cigar. He has an urge to stuff another one in his mouth even before this one is finished. His left hand painfully grasps the steering wheel while the right one fondles the portable police light next to him. The traffic is not too heavy, but he finds himself weaving in and out of cars going way too slow for his liking. As he fingers the police light, he contemplates putting it on the roof and turning on his siren. He can do that, but if someone catches him he'll have to explain. He'll have to explain that his friend is in terrible danger because he's watching a bad movie.

He'll have to explain that this movie is a life threatening movie. He'll have to explain that this movie jumps out and attacks the audience.

On the other hand, it's certainly worth the embarrassment if he actually can save Juniper's life. He grasps the light and picks it up. Then again, Juniper promised not to look at it. Is that good enough? Will the movie attack someone when it's just lying around? Wooden stops and thinks how ridiculous this all sounds. He thinks back to the fire at Henson's place. Could he have imagined it? With flames all around and smoke in his lungs and eyes, could he have hallucinated the entire episode with the film? It doesn't seem so, but maybe he just got tangled up in the film. The fire was raging, the projector was going, the film reel was spinning. He panicked, fell into the projector, got tangled up in the film, and freaked. Could that have been it? He puts the light back down on the seat. That's not what he remembers, but celluloid doesn't attack people. It's just absolutely, one hundred percent, indisputably, unconditionally not possible. He tosses his cigar out the window, still lit and still with a good amount left to burn, and lights up another. He presses on the gas, swerves around a few cars and runs a few red lights. His foot hurts.

Wooden pulls around a corner and up to the curb and parks. He gets out and looks up at the multistory building of Trilby Laboratories, Inc. At the exact moment that he looks up, there is a tremendous explosion and the windows of the seventh story blow out, showering tinted glass on the sidewalks below. Wooden's heart sinks. He propels himself forward on aching feet and into the Trilby building.

The fire engine and ambulance sirens grow in the distance as two separate caravans of rescue vehicles converge on the Trilby building. The fire engines raise their ladders in a mournful salute as fire hoses pour streams of water on the sizzling seventh floor wreckage. Fireman rush in as do paramedics. Survivors are carried out carefully. Others are rolled out slowly but unceremoniously. Brent Wooden gnashes his cigar into bits of soft paper and moist tobacco as Terry Juniper is rolled out slowly but unceremoniously.

Chapter 27

"Chief, this is big. Bigger than both of us. Bigger than the department. This is big." Wooden is pacing back and forth in Police Chief Sorrington's office while Sorrington squirms uncomfortably on his big leather chair behind his big mahogany desk.

"What do you mean 'big'?"

"Big. Like real big."

A pause with more uncomfortable squirming. "I don't follow."

"These deaths. It's a plot or something. I don't

know. It's not just a killer. Not even a serial killer. I don't
know. It's big."

"So what is it exactly?"

"I don't know. Aren't you listening? I don't know."

Sorrington lowers slightly his soprano pitch in an
attempt to sound fatherly and comforting. From this little man
in his overwhelming chair and desk, he sounds more like a
little boy consoling a stuffed bear. "You've been through a lot,
Brent."

At the use of his first name in this unfamiliar tone of
voice, Wooden stops his pacing to look at Sorrington.
Sorrington continues. "You've rescued a man from a burning
building--saved his life, in fact." A pause. "And you've just
had a friend die. You're under a lot of stress." Another pause as
if to check some mental notes for this obviously rehearsed
speech. Wooden imagines a typewritten department form letter
going through Sorrington's mind with blanks where he can fill
in the appropriate information: "I know that (friend's name) was
very close to you. I know that this case has taken on personal
meaning, (name of officer). But with your (number of years on the
force) years on the force, you certainly know that the
department can't allow an officer to investigate a case where

(he/she) has a personal involvement. Especially a case as (volatile, political, important, publicized, other) as this one.

"Also, I believe that you need a rest to recover both physically and emotionally. That's why I'm recommending (5 days, 10 days, one month, six months) leave with pay so that you can (get your act together, rest and rehabilitate, let loose, put yourself under the care of a physician, undergo a thorough psychological investigation). (Optional:) We'll be looking forward to your return. (Cast eyes downward as a sign of sympathy)."

Wooden looks at Sorrington. "Ah, fuck you," he says and continues his pacing.

Sorrington's voice rises in anger above its normal soprano. His freckled face turns all red. "Listen, Wooden, you're off this case! Go home, have a drink, get your rocks off, do what you need to relax so we can get you back when we need you."

"You need me now! You going to just let this case drop? People are getting killed out there!"

"Of course we're not letting it drop. We've got someone to take it over. You're going to brief him."

"Who?"

"Bob Simmons."

"Simmons? That little hamster? That guy enjoys this stuff! He'll keep it going just to have more bodies to examine."

"He's here and you'll brief him and then you'll go. Understand?" Wooden doesn't answer. Sorrington hits the intercom button on his desk. "Peggy? Send in Simmons."

Bob Simmons enters, his little curly black head flopping back and forth as he walks, a notepad in his hand, a pencil behind his ear. His mouth and eyes alternate between the serious, studious look that he knows is appropriate for a murder case and the wide eyed glee of being in charge of his first serial homicide investigation. "Chief." He nods at Sorrington who nods back. "Brent." He nods at Wooden who grimaces and forces air through flared nostrils which, had it gone through his vocal cords instead, would have formed very unflattering words. Simmons sits in a chair in the corner, pulls his pencil from behind his ear and places it directly above his notepad, hovering. With his thick neck jutting forward he appears like a squat vulture, his dark eyes flitting between the two of them, ready to devour any carrion thrown in his direction.

Sorrington: "Okay, Wooden, begin."

Wooden begins reluctantly. "There have been several murders."

Simmons begins scribbling furiously. Sorrington looks at him. "We know that. Come on."

Wooden continues. "Okay . . . Uhh . . . Victims are from all walks of life, all incomes, all age groups. No connection there."

"Walks . . . Groups . . . No connection . . ." Simmons mutters to himself while scribbling.

Sorrington is impatient. "We have your reports, Wooden. We need to know what's not in them. Leads. Hunches. New information."

Wooden swallows. "The movie."

Sorrington: "What's it called?"

Wooden: "*Horror Flick.*"

Simmons: "Horror what?"

Wooden: "Flick! Flick!"

Sorrington: "So you think the killer has some connection to this movie."

Wooden: "I think the killer is the movie." He pauses for effect. It works. Simmons stops his scribbling and looks up at him. Sorrington's face screws up.

Sorrington tries to hold back his impatience. "So what exactly are you saying?"

"I'm saying that there's something going on beyond
. . . beyond what we normally know about."

"Like what?"

"Like there's something about this movie that I can't
explain."

"You mean, of course, that you can't explain the
brilliant special effects. Or the wonderful acting. Or how a
bunch of magnetic particles on a strip of cellophane shows up
as moving pictures and high fidelity sound. Right?"

"I mean the goddamn film attacked me."

Bob Simmons resumes his frantic scribbling, wide
eyed.

Sorrington shakes as he continues to hold back his
anger. Through clenched teeth, "Exactly how did this film
attack you?"

"It wrapped itself around my wrists." Wooden holds
his wrists out for illustration.

Simmons looks up then down, muttering "around
wrists . . ."

"Wrapped around your wrists. You didn't get
tangled in it; it wrapped around your wrists."

"Exactly." He clears his throat. "And, uhhh . . . the

face on the screen stared at me. I mean it looked at me."

"On the projection screen."

"Yes."

"A face on a film is projected on a screen and you find that somehow bizarre."

"It wasn't projected. The thing actually looked at me. The damn thing looked at me!"

Simmons looks up. "Ahh . . . excuse me. What face are you talking about?"

Both Wooden and Sorrington look at Simmons. Sorrington explodes. "The goddamn face on the movie screen!" He snaps his face toward Wooden. "Are you talking psychic gobbledygook here Wooden?"

"Yes! Damn it! Something's going on! Something evil or occult or just fucking weird! It's time we face that and act on it!"

Like a thermometer, the red rushes up Sorrington's neck to his chin, to his mouth, to his eyes, to his forehead, to his scalp. "I told you no bogeymen! I will not have bogeymen in this department!"

"You've already got them! Face it! The bogeymen are here, they're there! I didn't put them there! Now what do

we do about them? What do we do before they kill again?"
Wooden spins around, and storms out, slamming the office
door behind him. Simmons looks after him, mouth agape.
Sorrington's hands are clenched in tight little balls; his skin is
nearly aflame.

Wooden marches angrily through the police
building, down the stairs, into his car and speeds away. His left
foot hurts badly.

Chapter 28

Wooden takes his anger out on his gas petal as his car speeds down the street. He'd like a cigar, but his hands are clutching the steering wheel too hard for him to peel one off. Up ahead he sees a video store and spontaneously hits his brakes. The car screeches painfully, slowing down enough for him to careen the car into the driveway and just avoid the Buick with the old lady whose eyebrows nearly launch themselves off her face while her heart misses several precious beats. He whips into a, luckily empty, parking spot and catches his breath.

Before entering the store, Wooden sits in his car and removes his left shoe and sock to massage his aching foot. He looks at it closely. On the side is a tiny, red insect bite. It is a small lump rising from the surface of the foot with red spreading outward like a tiny volcano. He touches it and the pain is sharp. A small drop of blood forms at the head. He wipes it off with his finger, puts his sock and shoe back on, and gets out of the car.

In the store, he rushes to the horror section and looks under 'H'. The film isn't there. Night is falling and as darkness settles, weary people returning from work begin to jam the little store, each looking for their own passports to escape the real world. It doesn't help that this madman is frantically fingering each cassette in the horror section, jostling people and muttering loudly to himself. An elderly lady, a businessman, a teenage couple with spiked hair and torn T-shirts, a young girl--all approach the section but think better of it and retreat as this crazy man, arms flailing unnoticed at both sides nearly presses his nose against each title in order to read it clearly. A little girl with her mommy points at him. "Is that a homeless person?" she asks referring to Wooden's disheveled hair, dark circled eyes, unshaven face, and wrinkled clothing.

Her mommy ushers the little girl away quickly.

Wooden grumbles loudly, then sprints for the cashier's desk. "Do you have *Horror Flick?*"

The pimply-faced teenage cashier looks at him as he is checking out another customer. Putting on a well-practiced smile, the cashier replies, "Be with you in a minute, sir," and returns to helping the customer.

"There's a line," says one of the little old ladies that seem to have overrun the place. She is standing next to him, or more precisely below him, this tiny woman in the huge fur coat wrapped tightly around her in this seventy degree weather. Her voice is gruff with a slight snarl. Wooden looks at her and his right fist coils up, but he releases the expletives as a hot breath through his nostrils as he moves behind her.

The first man finishes and the old woman approaches the cashier. She reaches up to the counter and smacks a video down on it. The cashier takes it in his hands and starts to ring it up. Wooden stands behind her impatiently ringing his hands and scowling. "Is this a good movie?" asks the old lady.

The cashier looks at it. "Yeah. This is very good. I think you'll enjoy it." Wooden hops from foot to foot, his left one even more sore than before.

"It's not a dirty movie is it? Everything these days is dirty. Filthy. If it's dirty, I'm gonna bring it back and someone's gonna catch hell, I'll tell you that right now."

The cashier examines the box again. "Well, it does have some bad language in it, I think."

"Bad language like what? Like 'hell'? That's okay as long as it's used in a religious sense. Is it used in a religious sense?" Wooden stares down at this lady hoping his glare will heat her head so that she'll want to leave quickly.

"I don't know," says the cashier, "I can ask."

"Ask if it's got 'damn' or 'shit' in it, too. Those are the worst. I just won't listen to those words in my own home. It's disgusting."

"I don't know," replies the cashier. He looks around to call someone over.

"It's okay," Wooden jumps in. The old lady and the boy look at him. "It's a great movie. Take it."

The old lady looks at him with suspicion. "It doesn't have 'damn' or 'shit' in it?"

"Or 'cocksucker' or 'mother fucker'. It's a wonderful family movie. It's clean. It's entertaining. Two thumbs up."

The lady looks at him for a moment longer than turns to the cashier. "Better be, or someone'll have to deal with me." She reaches for her purse.

"A dollar thirty-nine," announces the cashier.

The woman fishes around in her wallet. "Do you take pennies?"

"Ahhh!" cries Wooden. He pulls out his wallet and slaps two dollars on the table. "It's on me. Go. Enjoy it." She stands there looking at him. "Go!" He waves his hands at her like brushing dust off a coat. She takes her video from the counter and scurries off and out the door, all the while eyeing him suspiciously.

"Do you have *Horror Flick?*"

"Yes sir. The last aisle on the left. A whole selection."

"No, no. I want a film called *Horror Flick.* It's an old film. A vampire film or something. It's a real bad film."

"We have lots of good films, sir. Maybe you'd like . . ."

Wooden's volume increases. "I want *Horror Flick!* The movie is called *Horror Flick.* Do you have it?"

The cashier types into the computer on the table. "It's out. Maybe you'd like something else?"

"No! I want *Horror Flick*. Where is it?" People turn and look at Wooden as his voice grows ever louder.

The cashier reaches below the table and subtly pushes a small button. "Can I suggest *Attack of the Killer Tomatoes* instead? It's a . . ."

"No damn it! Only *Horror Flick*. Maybe someone in the store has it." He turns around to face the customers, most of whom are looking at him at this point anyway. "Does anyone have *Horror Flick*?" There is a slight murmur but no reply. "Anyone? It's a movie. Does anyone have *Horror Flick*. It's dangerous! If you have it, give it to me! It's a dangerous movie! Your life is in danger!" The people look at each other, some beginning to crouch for the gunfire they feel is certain at any moment from this lunatic. They talk to each other in whispers and move in small, smooth movements.

There is a barely audible sigh as two uniformed police officers enter from the front door. The crowd's gaze turns collectively toward them, and Wooden sees their faces and turns also.

"Detective Wooden," says one, approaching him.

Wooden calms down, noticing for the first time the fears on the people's faces. He addresses the police officer. "Jim . . ."

"Smith. Jim Smith."

"Yes. Officer Smith. Jim."

Jim Smith puts one hand gently on Wooden's shoulder to guide him toward the door, keeping the other at his side by his holster. Wooden recognizes the tactic. And the irony. "How about we talk about this outside." Wooden doesn't resist Smith's gentle encouragement as they head slowly outside. The other officer remains inside to reassure everyone.

"So what's going on. We were called about a disturbance."

"I . . . Yeah. I was the disturbance."

"Everything okay? You want to talk about it?"

"Nothing to talk about."

"You sure? I know you've been under lots of pressure. Everyone in the department knows." Pause. "We all want to break something now and then."

"It's not that. It's . . . hard to explain."

"Look, forget about it. This never happened. No report, nothing. Go home. Relax. Okay?" Smith hands him a card. "Here's my number. You want to talk about it, give me a call." Wooden looks at it then puts his head down, weary. Smith pats him on the back as he trudges to his car, the insect bite on his foot throbbing. He stops for a moment, says "Sorry," then continues. He doesn't know if Smith heard him and figures it's just as well.

Chapter 29

Wooden straddles the edge of his bed, a whisky bottle in one hand, a shot glass in the other. He pours himself a drink and puts the bottle on the night table. With his free hand he tugs off his left shoe and struggles to get off his sock, spilling only a little on his pants and the bed. He slams back the shot, then leans over to inspect his foot. The insect bite is larger, redder, and more painful. It is the size of a dime now with a head of pus and blood. He touches it and pulls back, clenching his teeth. It's sensitive and it hurts.

In the drawer of his night table he fishes around until

he finds a tiny tube of some gooey antibiotic gel whose label
has worn off to reveal the shiny metallic foil underneath. He
dabs a little bit on the bite. It stings. He massages the sides of
the foot, as close as he can get to the bite without causing too
much pain.

What in the world is this, he thinks. He picks up his
shoe and looks inside. He turns it upside down. Something dark
is caught in the lining. He pulls the lining back and shakes the
shoe. A small sliver dislodges and floats downward, reflecting
dots and flashes as it twists in the light of the table lamp.

Wooden leans over for a better look at this dark
flake. He picks it up delicately by the corner and holds it up to
the light. It burns slightly. It's a frame of film. Of the film he
fought with in Henson's house. It's a frame from *Horror Flick*.
Rummaging through another drawer in the table he pulls out a
jewelry case. He snaps it open and shakes it until the gold band
inside drops out and into the drawer. He places the film clip
inside and shuts it. For good measure he wraps a rubber band
around it. Tightly. He places it on the night table then pours
another shot which he lifts to his tired mouth. Finishing, he lets
himself collapse onto the bed for a very fitful night's sleep.

Chapter 30

"Look, Detective Wooden, you really expect me to believe that?" Roger Herman rises out of his chair.

Wooden continues pacing in Herman's office, a soggy, unlit cigar drooping from his lips. "No. I don't know. I'm the detective in charge of this case. I can bring you down to the station and show you the records."

"And the records say that my film is killing people."

"No. The record says that people have been dying and the only connection is your film." Wooden stops. His eyes are lined with dark circles. His hair is combed back but strands shoot out in random patches. His clothes are clean and pressed but he looks rumpled within them.

Herman pauses as the two look eye to eye. "Detective Wooden. Over the years I and my film company have been attacked by all sorts of moral majorists, feminists, psychologists, fundamentalists, artists, and every other kind of ists. My films have been called psychotic, sexist, blood thirsty, racist, gratuitous and even oblong. I can even agree that some of my films are bad. Some even very bad. But none of my films is so bad that people die from watching it!"

"Not from watching it. You don't understand. This film reaches out and kills people. It's like it's got a mind. A personality. It's evil!"

Herman reaches down slowly toward his intercom button. Wooden shoots out his hand and grasps Herman's hand before it reaches the button. "I'm not a nut," says Wooden, looking into Herman's wary eyes. "I'm not going to peel off my clothes or sing old movie songs." Herman still looks wary. Wooden releases his grip. "I just need help. I know this all sounds crazy. I know I sound crazy. But that film has killed people . . . including a good friend of mine. That guy Henson who interviewed you and you gave him a copy? He almost died, too. I . . . I saved him. I . . . had to . . . uhhh . . . fight the film. Believe me. It reached out and grabbed me and tried to kill me too. I don't know what to tell you to make you believe me."

Herman takes his hand away from the intercom buzzer. "You don't have anything more convincing than just your word? No proof?"

"Only this." Wooden reaches into his pocket and pulls out his jewelry case. Carefully he takes the rubber bands off and opens it. He puts it forward to Herman.

"So what's this?"

"It's a clip from your film. It's the only piece that survived the fire at Henson's place. That I know of."

Herman steps backward nervously. "So what's it gonna do? Jump up and bite me?"

"I don't think so. Just touch it."

"Why?"

"It's hot. I mean it burns. Is that normal?"

Herman reaches over cautiously and picks up the film frame by the edge. "So it's a little hot. This is proof that it's haunted?"

"It's the best I can do."

Herman returns the film clip to the jewelry case in Wooden's still extended hand. "Detective, if that's the . . . ouch!"

"What?" Wooden leans over to see Herman's hand. A ragged cut on his index finger is leaking little droplets of blood. "There, see!" Wooden exclaims.

"So I cut myself on it. It's still . . ."

"You didn't cut yourself. It jumped up and bit you, just like you said."

Herman looks curiously at the ragged cut oozing blood. He thinks for a moment, then turns to Wooden. "Look, detective. Put yourself in my place. What would you think if some guy came to you with a story like this."

"A few days ago I'd have said he's bananas and I'd have called Security to take him away. Right now, I'd say, 'Here I am. What can I do?'"

Herman looks at his finger for a moment longer. He sighs heavily. "Okay, detective. Here I am. What can I do?"

Chapter 31

Wooden and Herman sit uncomfortably, their big frames centered on small, metal folding chairs in the small, simply adorned room. There are chairs lined up on both walls like the waiting room for some backwoods abortionist, thinks Wooden. At the end of the room is a glass counter with exotic charms and Tarot cards, small leather bound books and some drug paraphernalia which doesn't make Wooden feel comfortable at all. Behind the counter is a staircase. At the door is a small counter with a cash register and some mints and chocolates, not unlike a restaurant or small gift ship.

On the walls are a few psychedelic posters, a horoscope, a "know your mushrooms" chart, several diplomas, and a collection of autographed pictures of movie stars hung haphazardly and crooked, bumping crowdedly against each other. In the center is one of Reva Trantini signed, "Yours forever, Reva Trantini." The same famous evil visage stares directly at Wooden and he diverts his eyes downward and crosses his legs nervously. "So tell me again about this place," he says to Herman.

"I already told you."

"I know but each time you do, you'll remember other details. Maybe something'll come up that's important."

"Like what?"

"How the hell do I know."

Herman takes a deep, annoyed breath, and starts. "Okay. Like I told your friend, Trantini was an occult freak by the time I met him. I heard it happened gradually. After playing all those roles he began to believe in it. You know, it was the occult that made him a star so I guess he felt some obligation to it. Those books in the shelf--" Herman points at the glass counter. "They're witches books. Trantini carried one with him. Between takes he'd read it and reread it. Every night around midnight he'd have an appointment here. We'd have to plan it so we weren't shooting then, because no matter what, he'd be here.

"The lady who runs this place, Jasmine, used to show up at the shoot a lot, too. She was sexy in an odd, gypsy kind of way. There were rumors that he was screwing her, but at his age that would really take magic. If I thought this stuff would let me get it up in my seventies, I'd give up my whole business and buy all the witch books, Tarot cards, and crystal balls I could get my hands on."

At that moment, a terrifying, inhuman howl echoes from the floor above them. Herman and Wooden are quiet. They fidget some more in their chairs. After a minute, there are footsteps on the creaky wooden stairs behind the glass counter. A pregnant woman in a faded flower print sack dress comes down followed by a thin man clutching a muzzled poodle to his chest. The poodle's legs twitch and thrash as the man struggles to hold on to it. "Definitely a demonic possession. I believe it may be a Mayan wolf god but I really can't be sure," says the woman with a seemingly inappropriate cheerful smile.

The man's face wears a pained, fearful look. "What do I do?"

She sees the man's face and responds to it rather than to his question. "There's nothing to worry about. This thing happens all the time. Just put this powder in Foo-foo's meal twice a day." They reach the counter at the door. She hands the man a small medicine bottle from a pocket in her dress. "If she doesn't improve in about a week, give this man a call." She reaches into a card file below the counter and comes up with a business card in her hand. "Pet exorcisms are his specialty. I'm not really trained in that field. He's expensive but worth it." She reaches over to pet Foo-foo who growls deeply at her. She pulls her hand back but continues smiling. "She'll probably be okay in a week."

The man thanks her and walks out. As he passes the two men in the chairs, Foo-foo growls and snaps at them, her legs wriggling and thrashing. The man pulls her back closer to him and frowns an embarrassed apology. Herman and Wooden watch him leave.

"May I help you?" The woman at the counter turns to them and Wooden examines her features using his professional and expertly developed skills from years as a detective. Her breasts are huge! His initial thought that she was pregnant as she bounced down the stairs was wrong. The formless dress hid her shape, and her large breasts hung low, braless, on her chest, puffing her dress out in maternity fashion. But now he can see that at rest, the dress falls deeply between the two orbs. "May I help you?" repeats the woman with no sign of impatience.

Wooden looks up, embarrassed that she may have noticed him staring at her. Herman flushes, too, also embarrassed. "We're looking for . . ." squeaks Herman, then clears his throat and tests it with a few deep "hmmm . . . hmmm . . ." sounds. He stands up. "We're looking for Miss McKittrick."

"That's me."

"No. That can't be. Unless you've truly discovered the fountain of youth. I knew a Miss McKittrick about, oh, twenty-two years ago. You must be only about . . ."

"Twenty-two. You're probably looking for Jasmine."

"Yes! Jasmine."

"I'm her daughter. Buttonwillow. Buttonwillow McKittrick." She thrusts out her hand with a great smile, her body bouncing as she does so, like an bubbly little girl.

Herman takes her hand. "I didn't know Jasmine was

married."

"She wasn't."

Herman looks down, embarrassed. "Oh, I . . ."

"It's okay. It was the sixties, you know. Free love
and all that. She was such a good mother I didn't need a dad."
She extends her hand to Wooden who takes it. He notices that
her arms, and her legs are thin, in fact shapely. They form a
strange contrast to her sizeable breasts. Her body intrigues him
as her dress wraps around to outline parts momentarily as she
moves. And the parts that do show he finds somehow very
sensuous even if it's only a bit of shoulder or a calf. He feels
like a boy given a present with some of the wrapping torn off
so that the contents are partly visible. He wants to tear the
wrapping off completely and blushes at the thought. She seems
to know what he's thinking and her smile brightens slightly.
Then again, maybe she does know what he's thinking, he
thinks, and blushes again.

"Where can we find your mother?" asks Wooden.
"We need to talk to her."

"That's going to be difficult."

"She's dead?" asks Wooden apprehensively.

"No. She'd be easier to reach if she were. She

disappeared over Bermuda a few years back. She was going
there to close a business deal."

"A business deal?" Herman squints in doubt.
"Doesn't sound like the same woman I knew who ran this little
palm reading boutique twenty-two years ago."

"It is. She got into phone services a few years back.
You know, dial up for your horoscope or find out where Elvis
was last spotted or which celebrity is a space alien love child. It
really took off. She became president and CEO of Telepath
Communications, Incorporated. It became a multimillion dollar
operation. One day, on the way to Bermuda, she just
disappeared."

Herman and Wooden look skeptic. "Oh not a
Triangle disappearance--nothing supernatural. She just wanted
to give it all up and lead the simple life. That was Mom's way.
So she just started a new life somewhere--didn't let anyone
know. I'm sure she's telling fortunes and reading Tarot cards in
some small town.

"She left the business to me. I sold it all off. I'm
more into research. That's what I do here. And some clinical
work. But mom--I couldn't tell you where to find her now."

Herman and Wooden look at each other in

disappointment. Wooden looks back at Buttonwillow. "We need to talk to her. It's extremely important."

"Maybe I can help you. I'm a psychic and certified occultologist. All of Mom's previous customers have been happy with my services. She taught me all I know."

"It's about a film I made twenty-two years ago," says Herman.

"This is very strange, I should warn you," says Wooden.

"Strange is my business," she says in a mock macho detective voice. "Believe me, I've heard strange. I'm used to it. This sounds like a long story, though. Why don't we go upstairs to the lounge area."

Wooden looks toward the door. "Shouldn't you lock the door? What if a customer comes in? Or a thief?"

She shrugs her shoulders nonchalantly. "I'll know," she says and walks up the stairs. Herman and Wooden follow, watching the gift wrapping cling and sway, revealing and hiding.

On the second floor they enter a nicely decorated lounge with tasteful wooden desks, antique lamps, and leather chairs and couches. The walls from floor to ceiling are lined with shelves of books, many of them old and expensive

looking. They cover such bizarre topics as spiritual

awakenings, out of body experiences, and UFOs but also

include more traditional topics such as child psychology and

gravitational physics.

The men make themselves comfortable. "Mind if I

smoke?" asks Wooden.

"Very bad for you--physically and spiritually.

Tobacco has a very strong Kirlian aura that tends to negate

your own aura. Why not try this instead." She reaches into a

drawer in a table and pulls out something wrapped in tissue

paper. She unwraps it and extends to him three brownish red

things like shriveled fingers. "It's a Gotu kola stick. You chew

on it."

Wooden takes one apprehensively. "It's not a

hallucinogenic, is it?"

"No. It's completely legal, detective. You just chew

on it."

Wooden puts the strange twisted thing into his

mouth and bites. A flavor a little like ginger and a little like

licorice floods his mouth. He coughs and swallows. Tears fill

his eyes. He coughs some more.

"Chew on it, don't bite it. Anyway it takes some getting used to." She puts the remaining fingers back in a drawer.

Wooden begins describing the events of the past two weeks. Unconsciously, he puts the Gotu kola stick in his mouth and sucks on it. In small doses it's not so bad.

As he talks he watches Buttonwillow--her round, cherubic face framed by wispy blonde hair with a ragged edge falling just below her shoulders. He watches her puffy, pouty lips and her wide inquisitive eyes. And her breasts. He finds his eyes drawn to them and he feels himself getting aroused. He forces himself to concentrate on what he is talking about--the murders, the film, his heroic struggle, the explosion and death of his friend.

When Wooden finishes, Buttonwillow McKittrick looks up at the ceiling, thinking. "That's strange."

After a mute moment Wooden asks "Did your mom ever mention Trantini?"

"He used to visit her regularly and she'd come to the shoots to watch him," adds Herman.

Buttonwillow purses her pouty lips and scrunches her eyes in thought. "She did sometimes mention him--he'd pop into her head for no reason I could see. I mean I'd be talking to her and she'd make some comment about what a dashing man he was or his intensity. We'd be talking about the weather or some boy I was dating or something completely unrelated and she'd come up with this total non sequitur about Reva Trantini. And that would be it. We'd finish what we were talking about and there'd be no more mention of him. I do remember I'd get some unusually complex resonances from her for a minute and then they'd disappear."

"Like bad vibes?" asks Herman.

"We don't call them 'vibes'. The terminology is 'psychic resonances'." She looks at Herman, her smile dimming for just a moment. "Anyway, not good or bad. Just complex. Maybe good and bad. They came and went so fast I couldn't really experience them fully. Know what I mean?"

Herman and Wooden shake their heads even though neither has any idea what she means.

"Anyway, it didn't happen that often, really. Maybe once a year. Twice a year."

There is a pause as Herman and Wooden expect Buttonwillow to go on, but she doesn't. Herman looks at her. "So what do we do?" He looks back at Wooden. "I mean I'm still not convinced this is anything but coincidence or the work of a very stressed out imagination." Wooden looks at Herman angrily. "But I'm willing to go along with it and help out if I can," he adds. "Show her the film clip."

Wooden pulls out the jewelry case and hands it to Buttonwillow. She looks at it. "Why don't we take this to my lab upstairs." They follow her up the staircase to the third floor where it ends at a room full of beakers and test tubes, Bunsen burners, computers, spectrum analyzers, and all other sorts of fancy equipment. On the walls here are shelves filled with carefully labeled and categorized bottles of chemicals. In the center of the room is a table on which a small laser is aimed at a test tube holding bluish-green substance. Two electrodes rise out of the tube and are connected to a display which beeps every few seconds and increments a number on the screen. She walks over to the table.

Herman looks around. "Where's your bubbling cauldron with newt eyes and toad lips?"

"Don't laugh. Witches were the scientists of their day. They experimented and came up with a lot of good medicines that still beat out anything on the market today. Only people are too prejudiced to try them. Anything today's scientists can't understand they figure is un-understandable. It's really just that there hasn't been a way of creating the right experiments or describing these phenomena mathematically.

"Not that I'm against science. Now we can use science to distill the chemicals from witches brew so that we can use pure dichlorobenzene or sodium methanol instead of newt eyes or toad lips."

Wooden and Herman nod at each other, impressed.

Buttonwillow catches their exchange. "I have a degree in biochemistry from Berkeley," she comments as explanation. She begins fiddling with a microscope on the table. "Anyway, most scientists are too rigid in their thinking. We can use things we don't yet understand. Look at aspirin. No one knows how that works, but we use it. And it works great-- for headaches, muscle aches. Now they find it works against heart disease and colon cancer. But what is it? It's just a derivative of the spirea shrub. Witches knew about it."

She takes the film clip out of the jewelry case and puts it on a slide and slips it under the microscope. She adjusts the focus. "Most scientists are men and men are just too rigid. Generally, that is. Of course, it makes sense from an anthropological point of view. After all, procreation depends on the male being rigid, right?" She turns to look at them. They look at her and shrug uncomfortably. "Anyway, that's another discussion altogether."

"So what can you tell?" asks Herman. "From the film clip?"

"It's a clip from a film. I need to run tests on it to see if anything comes up--some spiritual attachment or something. Of course if all the films and videos are being destructive then either they're all haunted, which is pretty difficult to believe given the probability, or the film's concept or theme or essence, if you will, is haunted. That would be something new. Of course, in this business you always find new things. That's the fun of it."

"Can I see it?" asks Wooden.

"Sure."

Wooden goes to the microscope and squints into it.

"What do you see?" asks Herman.

"It's Trantini. A single frame of Trantini's face like the one I saw on the projector at Henson's house. Just staring at me." Wooden continues looking. Suddenly, "Whoa!" Wooden backs away from the microscope, struggling to breath as if the wind were knocked out of him.

"What is it?" asks Herman.

Wooden convulses a couple of times with a sharp squeaking sound before he is able to suck some air back into his lungs. "It moved!"

"What exactly did it do?" asks Buttonwillow.

"It . . . Ummm . . . It . . . stuck its tongue out at me."

There is a pause. Buttonwillow begins laughing softly. Herman just turns away. "Shit," he says, disgustedly.

Wooden looks down, trying to regulate his breathing. He sits down and Buttonwillow comes over to him, rubbing her hand on his back reassuringly. "It'll be okay," she says like a mother comforting a little boy on the loss of his pet turtle. His breathing begins to slow. "So what do you want me to do?" Buttonwillow looks at Wooden.

"You look into this. Find out what ghosts or demons or goblins or whatever are haunting it. And also how to stop it. And Roger, you . . . you, uhhh . . . I don't know. Do what you can. I'm going to rent every damn copy of this film that I can find. Any questions?" Buttonwillow and Herman look at each other. "Okay. I'll call you both regularly to find out what's going on. Buttonwillow . . ." He pauses. "What do your friends call you for short?"

She looks at him, puzzled. "Buttonwillow."

"Okay . . . call me regularly with what you find. I assume you can devote full time to this--it's extremely important. Obviously."

"Obviously. I'm sure my clients can wait. Besides, this seems fun."

"And dangerous," adds Wooden.

"And dangerous," echoes Buttonwillow nonchalantly. "There is one other thing," she says.

"Oh?"

"I charge a hundred an hour plus expenses for something like this. With one day's work--eight hundred dollars--up front."

Wooden turns to look at Herman.

"Of course," sighs Herman who takes out his wallet and looks in it. "My checkbook is in the car."

"I take Mastercard, VISA, American Express, and Diner's Club."

"Of course."

Chapter 32

"Simmons, here."

"Simmons, this is Wooden. What's going on with the *Horror Flick* murders?"

"First, stop calling them that. The chief hates it."

"So is the chief listening in to phone calls now?"

"No, but . . ."

"Then don't worry about it. What's going on?"

"Second, you're off the case. In fact you're on R and R. Forget about the case--it's mine now."

"Come on, Simmons. Don't be an asshole. What's

going on?"

"Don't call me an asshole. You expect to get information if you call me an asshole?"

"Forget it. What's going on?"

"Lookit. You just called me an . . ."

"Okay! I'm sorry. I'm sorry I called you a fucking asshole!"

"A fucking asshole? Did you say fucking? First asshole, now fucking asshole."

Wooden pauses to take a deep breath and calm down. He applies his best Dale Carnegie principles. "Sorry, Simmons. I'm just a little high strung--you know that. I know you're doing a good job on the case--you're a good cop." Wooden turns his face from the phone and makes a vomiting gesture. "But it was my case before, and I'm curious what's happening. Maybe I can give you some pointers that'll help you solve the case."

"I don't need pointers." Simmons sounds like a hurt little boy. "Anyway there's nothing happening." The little boy is bored. "Seems like everything stopped after you left the case. Coincidence?" Simmons draws out the last statement teasingly.

"What? You think . . ."

"Just kidding. Just kidding. Jeeze. Can't you take a joke?"

"About homicide?"

"Anyway there's nothing to tell. Five deaths in ten days, then four days of nothing. Maybe the killer just got bored. Maybe he got run over by a bus."

"Not this killer."

"You still think it's some bogeyman, huh? Back from the dead. Whoooooooo . . ." Simmons makes a shrill, wavering "ghost sound" into the phone.

"Look Simmons, if you had any . . ." Wooden stops himself, grits his teeth, and tries to remember how to win friends and influence people. "Thanks, Simmons. If I think of anything that can help you, I'll let you know."

"Sure. Thanks." Simmons hangs up.

"Yeah, thanks bozo." Wooden dials another number.

"This is Herman."

"Wooden here. I wanted to know if you found anything."

"No. And I want you to know something."

"What?"

"I'm not doing this for any goddamn altruistic

reasons. I don't believe in anything but the almighty dollar, and if someone's released my film to video without my knowledge, or my banker's knowledge, then they're going to feel my full wrath, be they human or non, living, dead, or living dead. They'll hear from my lawyer and no force in this universe can withstand the fury of a Hollywood attorney. Comprende?"

"Sure. But if you find anything, you'll let me know."

"You'll be the third to know. I promise." Herman hangs up. Wooden dials a third number.

"Hi Brent."

"How'd you . . . never mind. How's the research going?"

"Well I ran some traditional chemical tests and they came up negative, but I did some Kirlian photography and the pictures are phenomenal. It just about burned through the photography paper. Now I'm looking for radiation at different parts of the spectrum. Certain wavelengths can be signatures for particular spirits or spirit types."

"Uh huh."

"Also, I'm personally picking up pretty strong resonances when I enter a trance state. I've been trying to channel them through me but I can't seem to direct them, you know?"

"Uh huh."

"Also, I picked up some books at the library. You familiar with 'Dimensional Connections of the Spirit' by Hoensnecker?"

"Unn Unn."

"Well, you should read it. He theorizes that we exist in multiple dimensions and have images in different planes. Kind of like shadows on a wall. Our bodies in this three-dimensional universe are just shadows of our full multidimensional selves. That's what Einstein was talking about. Hoensnecker goes beyond that to surmise that dying is like a big light--you know how people who have a near death experience report seeing a big light? Well, this light wipes out your shadow in one dimension but not necessarily in all of them. When you communicate with the dead it's because they're existing in another dimension. Hoensnecker even proposes that it's possible to divert your shadow, combine it with other objects or 'morph' it. There's a plethora of possibilities."

"Uh huh." There is a pause. "So . . . I, uhh . . . don't exactly see where this gets us."

"It gives us a basis."

Hesitantly, "Okay." Another pause. "A basis for what?"

"For an astral projection."

"A what?"

"A haunting. Someone's essence is projected into the film."

"In each film?"

"I don't know I'm figuring this out as I go along. Maybe the spectral analysis will help. I also have Agathalzer helping."

"Aga who?"

"Agathalzer. My spirit guide in the astral plane. I made contact with her, and she's talking to her connections there. If someone there is doing this, she'll find out. She was a private detective. Worked for the pharaohs in Egypt around three hundred B.C."

"Oh."

"Of course, there are a lot of people in the astral plane--most of the dead from the beginning of time. Don't expect her to yield anything too soon."

"Of course not." Wooden rubs his head and wonders

if maybe he has gone fishing permanently. "Anyway, let me know when you or your astral friend find anything."

"Will do, boss. By the way, what did you say was the name of this film?"

"*Horror Flick.*"

There is an anxious pause at Buttonwillow's end. "Oh no. How could I have forgotten the name? I knew it rang a bell."

"What?"

"It's on TV tonight."

"What?"

"The movie. *Horror Flick.* It's being shown on TV tonight."

"Are you certain?"

"Channel Forty-four. Slime Theater. They show old, campy horror films. It's a local show. It goes on in . . . twenty minutes! It was a change of schedule. They just announced it. Damn! I didn't even think . . ."

"Can this spirit, this entity or whatever kill over TV? I mean can it kill viewers?"

"I . . . I don't know. I didn't think of that. I suppose it depends how strong the spirit is. From what you've told me, it's very strong."

"Damn! I've got to stop the broadcast."

"What can I do?"

"Just keep working and figure out how to stop this thing from killing again."

"Be careful," whispers Buttonwillow. But Wooden has already hung up.

Chapter 33

"Used to be a cop, myself, you know." The white-haired security guard plods slowly down the long, barren hallway. The hallway seems to stretch to forever, lit by an infinite progression of long fluorescent bulbs. Everything is sterile white--white tile floor, white walls with white, wooden doors. White light from white light bulbs.

The guard's uniform is blue and gold, neatly pressed and starched, but too large for his old, shrinking body. It crinkles and crackles with each careful step he takes. Wooden speeds up and slows down, circling the man and impatiently attempting to prod him. The man's pace continues undisturbed and with great deliberateness. "What did you say you do?" asks the guard.

"What?"

"For a living!" The old man doesn't hold back his disdain at Wooden stupidity.

"I'm a cop."

"Oh yeah? Me too. I *used* to be a cop, that is."

"Listen, it's important . . ."

"Sure it's important. Protecting the public is very important. Did I mention I arrested Dillinger?"

"I've got to get to the broadcast room. Maybe you can . . ."

"Sure thing." The guard's voice drones on slowly. "Dillinger. Fought him like the dickens. Hand to hand. Slugged him in the jaw." The guard's voice drones on. "Dillinger's got a glass jaw I found out. I had some right cross, too." He stops and looks upward, reminiscing. "Course I was a youngster back then." Another pause. "Know how old I am now?"

Wooden looks nervously at his watch. "Eight thirty nine!"

"Eight hundred thirty nine? You joking me, boy?

I'm old but I'm not Methuselah."

"No, it's eight thirty nine. The time. Eight thirty nine. O'clock. It's already nine minutes into the movie."

"What movie?"

"The movie I've got to, uhh . . . see."

"Hmmm . . . " The man stops suddenly. "Here."

Wooden looks around but it's a hallway with nothing that looks like the door to a broadcast studio. "Where?" he asks.

"Here," the old man repeats and pushes open a door with a little blue spread-legged man on it. "Don't go nowhere." The guard disappears into the men's room.

No, thinks Wooden. He looks at his watch again. Eight forty-one! When does that scene occur? The one with the face. Five minutes. Twenty minutes? Shit! He looks down the hallway to see lots of doors and a staircase leading to several other floors. He jumps up and down. Come on, come on, old man. Empty your stupid bladder. Oh I hope you don't have prostate problems. Oh, please God, don't let him have prostate problems! Wooden slumps against the wall.

Chapter 34

Roger Herman, his wife Audrey, and his two kids, Jennifer and Patrick, finish their evening dinner. The smooth, polished, black Lucite table is cluttered with dishes and glasses containing half-eaten meals and half-drunk drinks. Napkins cover most of the food like blankets covering the dead in a military hospital. Elizabeth, their maid, is a large woman with blotchy brown complexion. She enters quietly through swinging doors of ornate wood. Her apron is too small to cover much of her abundant body. She picks up the dishes and returns them to the kitchen to be cleaned, disappearing through those same ornate doors.

"Dad," asks Patrick. "Can we watch your movie with you tonight?" His round cheeks bulge out of his round, cherub face.

"No." Herman stands up to make his way to the den and its television set.

"Why not?" asks Jennifer. She twists and pulls at the long brown hair that frames her long, narrow face.

"Because it's not for you. Don't you have homework tonight?"

"No," they sing in unison.

"I'll bet this movie's got people who get their arms pulled off and there's all blood and guts and stuff like hanging out all over." Patrick smiles. The two-tooth gap in the front is emphasized by the remaining large, white teeth in his big smile.

"I'll bet it's got people doing it," says Jennifer. She forms a circle with her left hand and moves her right index finger back and forth through it. Patrick and Jennifer giggle.

"Children!" says Audrey. She fixes them with a stern look that they easily ignore.

"No homework at all?" asks Herman. The kids shake

their heads. "Well, you ought to. Anyway, you need to take showers tonight."

"We took showers last night," replies Jennifer, skipping around the table. Her hands hold on to the sides of her cotton dress to keep it from parachuting up.

"Well take one again. You don't like being clean?" Their father is being unusually persistent. They run to him.

"Do we have to take a shower?" asks Patrick.

"Can't we see the movie?" asks Jennifer.

"Yes! No! Go!" Herman tries to continue on to the den, but his children circle, blocking his path. They are the Indians; he's the helpless wagon train.

Patrick starts to sniffle. "I don't want a shower!"

Jennifer adds, "I want to see the movie!"

"Do something. Clean up your rooms. Wash your clothes. I don't know. But you're not seeing the movie!"

Patrick breaks into tears which bounce from his large eyes, off his rounded red cheeks, landing in drops on his beach ball belly. Jennifer doesn't break into tears--she's too old for that. She shouts. "You're mean. You're the meanest dad!"

Just then, Audrey walks over with two large bowls containing mounds of ice cream swirling in thick, steaming fudge. One bowl in each hand, she places each under the nose of a child. Saying only a single word, "dessert," she walks backwards, leading the kids hypnotically back to the dining room like some sort of Pied Piper. They follow her, noses in the air. They forget the movie, and their terribly mean father, as they devour their dessert, leaving small white and brown puddles on the freshly cleaned Lucite table.

Roger Herman continues walking toward the den. Audrey catches up with him. "What was that all about?" she asks.

"The kids were being brats, that's what."

She looks at him, unconvinced. Her face is soft and simple. Her hair, brown and wispy with a touch of gray, is bound up in a soft pink cotton bandana. She was once a bit actress--not a very good one--but with a soft, sweet, beauty to her. That beauty got her a few more parts, and a few more invitations to the casting couch, than she otherwise might have had from her acting ability alone. Now, the softness and sweetness is still there, but after marrying Roger some thirty or so years ago, she quickly fell into the comfortable role of wife and then mother. Her figure grew fuller, her rear end expanded, her breasts began sagging, and little bags of flesh grew under her upper arms. Still, on occasion she can recapture that look at an important party or banquet. A little makeup and the right clothes can transform her for an evening.

"Okay, I'm tense," Herman continues. "A bad week. So I'm a little irritable."

"So does this movie have people doing it?" She smiles mischievously.

"No. It's a stupid little movie I made years ago. Someone released it illegally and I'm pissed off about it."

"How about if I meet you in the den in a few minutes and after the movie we can figure out a way to work off your tension." She smiles and gives him an exaggerated wink. He misses it. She moves in to kiss him.

"You'll bring some popcorn?"

"Of course," she says, annoyed. She wants to resume the kiss, but he turns and walks off to the den. Audrey sighs and returns to the dining room.

In the den, Herman sits on the big, soft couch in front of the television. The den, too, has walls of ornately carved wood. Very austere. Very expensive. Knick knacks and high priced trinkets inhabit the dark-wood-and-carved-glass cabinets that line the walls. A seventeenth century gold plated clock sits on a table in the corner, lifted by naked cherubs. It does not keep time, the spring having broken years earlier.

Roger Herman turns on the TV set. Several minutes later Audrey enters and settles beside him with a big metal bowl of popcorn. Herman reaches over to kiss her, grabbing a handful of popcorn as he does so.

After seemingly endless commercials and the insipid comments of a third rate actor in a cheap vampire outfit, the movie begins. Herman watches the dripping credits as they appear and fade from the screen as he remembers the accounts of the murders that Wooden related to him in detail. Ridiculous to think that his film suffers from some sort of demonic possession. That it can kill people. That's just . . . ridiculous. No other word for it. Ridiculous. Still . . .

Herman looks at his wife who takes her eyes from the screen to return his gaze with a smile. A pretty smile. A loving smile. Audrey turns back to the TV and puts a handful of popcorn in her mouth. He watches her.

"Audrey?"

"Yes?"

"I'd rather you didn't watch this film."

She finishes chewing her popcorn. "Yeah?"

"Yeah."

A pause as she puts another handful of popcorn in her mouth. She chews quietly, with grace. "Why not?"

"It's . . . it's a bad film."

"So?" muffled through popcorn.

Herman can feel an indigestion attack coming on. "It's really bad. I . . . I made it a long time ago. I'm . . . I'm embarrassed by it." He has a bad feeling about where this is leading.

"You're embarrassed by it? You love your bad films. We watch all your bad films and laugh at them. They're hysterical."

"This is really bad. Really, really bad."

She looks at his face and thinks about it. After all these years, she can read his emotions fairly well. "That's not it, Rog. There's something else."

"That's it. That's all. It's bad. Just don't argue. Please." The indigestion builds. He swallow a fistful of popcorn to absorb the burbling acids.

"That's not it. You're not telling me something. What is it you don't want me to see?"

"Nothing. What wouldn't I want you to see? You see

all my movies."

"But not this one."

"Not this one. Please. Don't ask any more. Please."

She thinks about it for a moment, examining various reasons and tossing them out until she hits one that feels right. "Are you in this film? Did you put yourself in it? Is that why you never released it?"

"No."

"You're doing something in this film. Something you don't want me to see, maybe?"

"Audrey!"

"That's it!" She's hit on it.

"That's ridiculous! Why would . . ."

"There's a sex scene. Right? Are you 'doing it'? Are you 'doing it' with your secretary? Is that it?"

"Audrey."

"I remember her. A sassy blonde tramp. With the squeaky voice and inch long finger nails. What was her name? Janet? Am I right?"

"Yes."

Her eyes water. "I'm right? That's why you don't want me watching. You and Janet . . ."

"You're right about her name. Janet. That was her name."

"So you remember her name. She meant something to you, didn't she?"

"No. She meant nothing. I swear."

"She meant nothing. That's supposed to make me feel better? It was a fling. A meaningless fling at my expense. Did you laugh at me behind my back?"

"No, of course not . . ."

"No, you wouldn't laugh. You felt sorry for me. For little old Audrey."

"Audrey. Sweet. There's nothing. No Janet. No sex. No nothing."

"Then why don't you want me to see this movie? What are you hiding?"

"Nothing!"

"Go to hell! You're hiding something."

"There's nothing. That's it. End of discussion!" Herman crosses his arms, refusing to look at her. Audrey sits for a moment, fuming, clutching the popcorn bowl with tight, clawing hands.

Herman's indigestion builds. The acids rise. His

throat burns. "Go! Out of here! You're not watching this!"

"I'll find out anyway!" Audrey turns to leave.

Herman reaches out and places his hand gently on the popcorn bowl. "Can you leave the popcorn?" he asks timidly. Audrey looks at him, releases her grip, spins around madly, harrumphs at the top of her lungs, and marches angrily out of the room.

Chapter 35

The security guard emerges from the men's room and slaps his wet hands on his stiff blue pants. They leave symmetric hand prints on either side. "Come on," he says and continues his slow plodding down the hallway. Wooden straightens up and walks after him. It's eight forty-four now. Fourteen minutes into the film. Minus commercial time.

"I was telling you about Capone."

"Dillinger."

The man stops. "I'll have some respect from you, young man!" He shakes his finger at Wooden. "I used to be a

police officer." He continues his plodding down the long
hallway. The harsh lights glare off the white walls and floor.
They pass many nondescript doors at regular intervals along
the corridor. The security guard abruptly begins various
reminiscences about his youthful police days, and just as
abruptly stops each one. In between stories are long, impatient,
anxious silences.

About two-thirds down the hallway they reach a
door marked "Broadcast Center". The guard begins to push it
open but Wooden throws himself at it and bursts into the room.
The guard shakes his head and turns to walk slowly back to his
front door post.

In the room is a wall of television monitors, about
twenty of them, each showing Reva Trantini strangling his
victim. Each picture is perfectly synchronized with each other
picture, creating a mirror within a mirror type effect. In front of
the monitors is a control table. The man at the table turns
around to look at Wooden. "Hey, man. Do you have
authority?"

"I'm a police officer." Wooden holds up his badge.

The man is a large man with a round belly peeking
out from under a tie-died T-shirt. His long, frizzy, gray hair is

tied into a pony tail that reaches to the small of his back. He appears to be in his fifties and his granny glasses inflate his eyes to twice normal size. The man rubs his grizzled face. "I guess it's a philosophical question, anyway."

"So where's the studio? Where's the Slime Theater studio?"

The man points all around the room. "This is it, man. All on tape."

"I have to shut you down."

"Hey man, I can't let you do that."

"Get up. How do I turn this off. Lives are at stake."

"More like profits, you pig! Just like Korea and 'Nam and Panama and Kuwait."

Wooden moves forward. "Look I don't want to use force, but I'm authorized to do so," he lies.

The aged hippie starts to stand up, his shoulders slumping forward, his belly pushed out, and begins chanting. "Hell, no, we won't go! Hell no, we won't go!" His hands clap along rhythmically.

Reva Trantini's face in all twenty monitors turns to stare out in its familiar hypnotic stare. Trantini says the words "You . . . are goink . . . to die." At the site of twenty threatening Trantinis behind the chanting hippie, Wooden panics and pulls out his gun.

The hippie quickly raises both hands over his head and begins moving out of the way. "You didn't get away with this in Chicago in Sixty-Eight! You won't get away with this now!"

"How do I shut this off!"

The hippie lowers one hand to point to a big switch on the table. "This."

Wooden looks at it. Reva Trantini looks at Wooden. More precisely, four of the twenty television monitors of Trantini in the upper right corner turn to stare at Wooden, an expression of anger forming slowly. Wooden reaches over to the switch. Abruptly, the hippie lowers one heavy arm swiftly into Wooden's arm, knocking it away and Wooden onto the floor. Wooden's gun, of course, goes spinning into the corner and under some machinery. Four of the Trantinis smile. The other sixteen continue staring banefully into space.

Chapter 36

Roger Herman stuffs mouthful after mouthful of popcorn into his face, gnashing and crushing each biteful as if it were his enemy. The emotions he unleashes with each shattering mastication are a mix of embarrassment at this singularly terrible film and anger at those who released it without his permission, denying him the profits to which he is rightfully entitled.

With tempered memories, Herman watches the bloody credits appear and waver out. He watches the wobbly trash can lid fly across the early evening sky. He watches

Lieutenant Zimba stiffly receive her diabolical orders from her commanding officer. He watches Reva Trantini suck the blood from his first victim. And he watches Trantini's face turn hypnotically toward him and proclaim, "You . . . are goink . . . to die."

As Trantini says this, Herman hesitates, mesmerized, his hand suspended in mid grab above the large bowl of popcorn. He stares out at Trantini's face, intrigued by it even though he has seen it countless times in old movies. It still fascinates him. It still captivates eerily.

As he watches the face, a hand--a large, hairy, muscular, rough skinned, mud caked hand--shoots quickly out of the bowl of popcorn and wraps itself firmly around Herman's wrist. Herman looks down. Before a sound can escape his lips, this hand wrenches Herman's arm down into the now seemingly bottomless popcorn bowl, slamming his face against the metal edge. His scream is muffled by a faceful of puffed kernels.

Herman doubles over on the couch, the popcorn bowl in his lap, his arm extended straight downward into it which should, by all the laws of physics and sanity, puncture through the bottom and into the couch between his legs.

Instead it vanishes into some hidden dimension at the pull of some other-worldly demon.

Herman slides off the couch, the bowl slamming against the floor, his arm still buried within it. His forehead is bruised and bleeding from the pressure against the bowl's rim. Herman tucks his knees under him, sucks in a breath, and heaves himself upright. His face rises out of the bowl and his arm is visible to the forearm. He pulls and strains until his wrist becomes visible with the bony fingered demon hand still clenched around it. The veins on his wrist bloat as his hand becomes numb without circulation. The demon hand pulls unexpectedly harder and Herman flies downward into the bowl, his face now buried in white corn. He grasps the bowl with his free hand and pushes, fighting. Slowly his head lowers, the corn filling his nostrils. He breathes out forcefully to clear his nose and mouth, but despite his efforts his head sinks deeper, and the swarming white morsels close in to cut off his air.

Chapter 37

"What was that for?"

The hippie, confused, looks down at Wooden. "I don't know. I'm a pacifist, man."

Wooden stands up. "Get away. I could arrest you!" Wooden reaches for the switch again. The hippie starts to back away, then swings again at Wooden, who blocks it and swivels out of the way. "What the fuck are you doing?"

"I don't know, man." The hippie lunges for Wooden and smashes a fist into Wooden's side. Wooden brings his fist up for a jab to the hippie's stomach, but the hippie, with

unusual speed, throws out his hand and wraps it around
Wooden's fist. With his other hand he grabs Wooden by the
neck, throwing his head against some equipment. A thin line of
blood oozes from a slash on the back of Wooden's head.
"Sorry, man. Must be having a bad flashback or something."
He smashes Wooden's hand against the controls. "Truly.
Sorry."

Wooden brings up his knee and slams it into the
hippie's groin. The hippie releases his grip and Wooden again
lunges for the master switch. The hippie snatches Wooden by
the shirt and spins him away from the controls. "This is, like
real weird, man. A definite bummer." He throws Wooden
against the wall. "Hope I'm not hurting you or anything."

Sprawled out against the wall, spread eagle, Wooden
looks up to see the fire alarm. Reaching up, he takes the little
hammer from the holder. The hippie sees it and runs over to
him but Wooden manages to break the glass and set off a loud
wailing alarm. The four Reva Trantinis that have been
watching take notice. They're angry.

The hippie picks Wooden up by the shirt. Wooden
swings at the hippie, but from his position it's hard to get much
leverage and the blow glances off the hippie's face. The hippie

throws Wooden into the corner where Wooden's gun slid.
Wooden reaches under the equipment, frantically attempting to
reach it. His arm flails, his fingers move quickly back and
forth, attempting to reach the gun.

The hippie walks over. "Man, are you okay?" he
asks.

Wooden feels something. He stretches his arm and
fingers, just making contact with the cold steel of the gun. The
hippie raises his foot. Wooden desperately wriggles his fingers,
attempting to get a grip. The hippie stomps down quickly and
Wooden pulls back his hand just as the hippie's sandaled foot
comes crashing to the floor. Wooden scrambles away toward
the master switch again, the hippie in pursuit and the four Reva
Trantinis grinning happily. The alarm rings screechingly.

The hippie reaches down and pulls Wooden up, his
face less than an inch from Wooden's. "This is, like, too
weird." The hippie then slams his knee into Wooden's groin.
Wooden lets out a deep, heartfelt groan. Still holding Wooden
up, the hippie wraps one large hand around Wooden's neck and
begins squeezing the life out. Wooden thrashes, kicking out
and slapping, but the hippie holds him off the ground and
Wooden can't get any force behind his assault which, as the air

goes out of him, weakens quickly.

"Man, oh man," cries the hippie, literally crying watery tears as he crushes the life from this drooping marionette. Wooden lets out a deathly hiss that ends abruptly. The four Trantinis smile. The sixteen Trantinis stare hypnotically. The alarm screams.

The door to the broadcast center swings open and the old security guard stands, silhouetted in the light from the outside hall. "What going on!" he shouts. He sees the hippie holding the limp body of Brent Wooden in his hands. The hippie turns to look at him. Two of the sixteen Trantinis turn quickly toward the security guard. The guard unstraps his pistol for the first time in thirty years, and points it in a nervous, wavering hand at the hippie.

"Stop or I'll shoot," yells the guard, shaking. His bladder is filling quickly. The hippie, a wild look in his eyes, drops Wooden's body which slumps to the floor. The hippie charges at the guard. The alarm screams. Two Trantinis look angrily at the guard. Four Trantinis look satisfied at Wooden. Fourteen Trantinis and numerous other Trantinis in television sets around the city stare demonically outward at men and women and children who all share some gruesome and terminal fate.

As the hippie lunges, the guard wraps his nervous finger around the trigger of the shaking gun and with surprising reflexes, pulls. The bullet sails past the rampaging hippie and squarely into the video tape copy of *Horror Flick* in the broadcasting equipment. All twenty Trantinis look in sudden anger at the sputtering, sparking equipment as it dies and their disappointed faces fade from the screens. The hippie stumbles and flies out and onto the aging security guard who both fall into a crumbled, shaking, and wet jumble on the floor. At the control panel, Brent Wooden coughs several times.

Chapter 38

Roger Herman's vision grows dark as his air supply is sapped by a bowl of popcorn. His left arm aches from the pull of the demon and his right arm aches from the struggle to keep his head from completely disappearing. His legs, his back, his arms all strain against the supernatural force that is pulling him toward oblivion. As determined as he is to survive, as valiantly as he struggles, his strength is limited, and gradually his face presses tighter and tighter into this bowl of death. The edges of his vision grow increasingly black as less and less precious oxygen reaches his brain.

At once, the grip on the other end disappears. He is thrust backward by the force of his own legs and arm which suddenly meets no resistance. He flies upward, flipping over the couch, and lands smack on his back. The television screen, like those in many other homes around the city, is abruptly filled only with grey and black snow and a steady electronic hiss.

In the living room, Audrey Herman sits angrily reading a book, unable to get past the first page. Her eyes continue to scan the same words over and over, but no meaning enters her brain. She repeats in her mind her argument with her husband. She pictures the secret film--the clandestine scenes that no one was ever supposed to see. In vivid, Technicolor detail, she sees his immoral liaison with that tramp, that home-wrecking slut.

Roger Herman storms into the room, his right hand holding a popcorn bowl, his left hand hanging limply at his side. His forehead is bleeding. His face is bruised. His arms are swollen. His pants are wet.

"What did you put in the popcorn?" His wild, booming, bellowing voice echoes throughout the large house. The children upstairs stop, frozen. His wife looks at him, frightened.

"What do you mean?" she asks quietly.

"What did you put in the goddamn popcorn?" This even louder than the last, the walls around him quivering. Herman's eyes turn quickly upward and a shrill, piercing howl bores through his gut and out his wide open mouth as he falls over onto his back and passes out.

Chapter 39

It's a surprisingly cold morning in Los Angeles, and it seems even colder to the huddled figure that sits on the sidewalk by the door at 1662 Vermont Street. A strong wind blows periodically, whipping up dust and trash and swirling them past the plain concrete and brick storefronts. The figure wears a thick down coat. As the wind starts up again, he pulls the collar up around his bruised neck and swollen cheeks. He closes his eyes, but the dust still manages to work its way in. His eyes tear. He waits, and eventually drifts off to sleep--not good sleep, but more sleep than he has had in this recent week.

Buttonwillow McKittrick walks briskly, confidently down Vermont Street, passing each concrete and brick storefront. The streets are virtually empty of people, and only occasional cars drive by. A long, red coat covers her from neck to ankle. Her wispy blond hair is whipped in all directions at once with each cold breeze, but when the breeze stops, her hair floats back to her head like feathers floating earthward. In her arms she carries a large pile of books and magazines. With each strong wind, she stops, pulls the stack tightly against her bosom, and steadies it with the bottom of her chin. When calm resumes, she continues her bouncy, cheerful excursion.

At her office door, she steps around a vagrant sitting on the sidewalk, asleep. Pressing her chin tightly into the stack of books and magazines, she carefully removes one hand to fish in her coat pocket. Finding a key, she opens the door and enters, placing the books and magazines carefully on the counter. Reaching into her jeans pocket, she finds some loose change. Grabbing it into her fist, she walks back outside and tosses it into the gap created by the vagrant's legs.

The sound of jangling change hitting the sidewalk awakens Brent Wooden. He blinks his eyes several times, dazed and not quite remembering where he is. After a few more blinks, the view comes into focus and his mind comes back to life. He looks up to see Buttonwillow turning back into her office. "Button . . ."

Buttonwillow turns back to the vagrant, a question mark in her expression. She looks closer. The vagrant pulls his head out of his collar. "Detective Wooden!"

"Brent," he replies softly.

She reaches down, takes his arm, and helps him to his feet. "What happened? You're okay?" He puts one arm around her shoulder as she leads him into the office and settles him into one of the folding chairs against the wall.

It's warm in the room, but he shivers for an instant. "I'm okay," he replies, after some delay, to her question. "I stopped the broadcast."

"I know," she says.

"How . . ." he begins to ask, then stops himself.

"You need to be cleaned up," she says to him. "And I've got some creams that will reduce the swelling and the pain. I'll be right down." She removes her coat and places it on the chair behind the counter. Underneath she wears another long, delicate, flower print dress. She starts toward the staircase.

"I could use a cigar if you have one."

"I'll see what I can do."

"Or a cigarette. A cigarette will do."

Buttonwillow nods, takes her books and magazines in her arms, and continues up the stairs. Wooden watches the long flowing dress wrap and unwrap her limbs with each step. When she has disappeared up the stairs, Wooden slips off his coat, slowly, to minimize the pain. He lets the coat fall over the back of the chair and sits, hands in his lap, waiting.

Upstairs he can hear Buttonwillow walking around, opening and closing cabinets; fishing through drawers. He looks around the room at the counter by the door with its mints and trinkets for sale, the cabinet at the far end with strange books and artifacts on display, the wall with the charts and posters and a diploma from the University of California at Berkeley. He looks at the wall across from him filled with pictures of celebrities. He scans across it to the one of Reva Trantini, and he stops involuntarily. He glances at the eyes. He shivers again. Outside, a strong wind starts up, rattling the flimsy wood frame door. Wooden's heart gives an extra beat. He looks down at the ground and blinks several times.

Buttonwillow appears once again at the bottom of

the stairs, damp rags draped across one arm. She holds a wicker basket of soaps and lotions and creams. She walks across the room, and without breaking stride, quietly takes the picture of Reva Trantini off the wall and places is gently, face down, on the counter. She continues over to Wooden. He looks up. She smiles at him and without a word begins applying soap and warm cloth and soothing balm to the bruises and wounds on his face. He watches her. Her face is bright and it warms him.

"I don't suppose you found a cigar?" he asks.

"This is better," she replies and holds up another Gotu kola stick.

Wooden begins to say something, then stops. She places it in his open mouth and he closes his lips around it. The juices begin flowing. It is rather soothing, he thinks.

Buttonwillow finishes with his head and neck. "So where else does it hurt?" she asks.

"This guy at the station. He pounded on my arm. My right arm."

Buttonwillow reaches over and unbuttons Wooden's shirt. Her fingers brush against his chest. They are soft. Warm. Comforting. She gently removes his shirt and lets it drop to the floor. She takes a cloth and applies one of the creams gently to his right forearm.

"He hit me in my left side."

She applies a lotion to his side.

"And my back." He turns to the side to give access to his back. She applies a pleasing salve.

"He kicked me in the groin."

Buttonwillow stops and looks at Wooden. He looks back innocently--a puppy dog. A soft smile grows on her face. She leans over to him and kisses him gently on the cheek. "I think you'll be okay now," she says. "Come on upstairs when you're feeling up to it." She gets up with her basket of creams and lotions, and walks gracefully up the stairs. Wooden watches her disappear.

Chapter 40

"Hellooooo."

"Up here."

Roger Herman lumbers up the steps to the third floor laboratory. His head appears first through the opening of the staircase, like a giant groundhog rising from the ground, looking around. Against the wall, on a lab bench, the frame of film sits in a Petri dish of yellowish fluid. Two thin metal probes in the fluid are attached to a oscilloscope and some sort of meter. The oscilloscope line is flat except for occasional short but violent blips like a seismograph recording a strong earthquake. The meter, too, is quiet except at those same times when the needle pins against the right side for several seconds before dropping back down.

Buttonwillow sits on a stool at a laboratory bench, her back to the staircase, hunched over, typing at a computer. Periodically, she stops typing to flip through pages of documents at her side. She runs her finger over a paper, stopping at particular passages, mumbles to herself, then continues her typing.

Wooden sits on a small plastic chair in a corner, his shirt is still off, revealing multiple cuts, lumps, and bruises on his bare chest. His left eye is swollen and centered in a dark black splotch. He swishes a Gotu kola stick back and forth in his mouth, pressing it alternately against each cheek, giving the impression of a small rodent in his mouth running from side to side in an attempt to escape.

"You look like shit," says Herman. "What happened?"

Wooden doesn't look up. "I had a close encounter." He fidgets uneasily in his chair, staring at his hands, folded in his lap.

"My film?"

"Yeah, but I was able to stop the broadcast."

"Well, *I* certainly appreciate that." Wooden looks up to see the sling on Herman's arm and the bloody bandage around the top of Herman's bruised face.

"And what happened to you?"

"A bowl of popcorn . . . uhhh . . . well, I was watching the movie and . . . let's just say something very strange happened and I wasn't sure I'd be around to talk about it today and I'm willing to believe that something beyond the ordinary is happening that's somehow associated with my film."

"It attacked you?"

"Yeah."

"Buttonwillow. Anything happen to you?"

Buttonwillow is thumbing through a book. "No," she responds without looking up, "I was working late last night. I didn't watch the broadcast."

"How about the newspapers?" asks Herman. "There must be some mention in the papers."

"I didn't see anything," responds Wooden. "That's why I figured maybe the film couldn't have an effect over TV signals. At least that's what I hoped. Maybe it just affected you and me."

"No, something happened last night. Something big. I could sense it while I was working." Buttonwillow continues to flip through the book and type notes into the computer.

"What, then? Why wasn't there something in the papers. If anything like what happened to me happened to others, it would have to be in the papers. Someone would have talked about it."

Buttonwillow looks up at him. "Did you talk about it? Did you call the papers?"

"No, but . . ."

"People don't like to talk about things they don't understand. They don't run to the papers with this kind of information. It is in the papers, though. You have to know where to look. You're not going to have front page headlines saying 'I was attacked by a goblin from the TV set'. In the tabloids, maybe. As a matter of fact, for all the junk in the tabloids, they're surprisingly on the mark sometimes."

Wooden looks at her. "So you're saying the news is in the tabloids."

"No, it's in the mainstream news, too. Look at today's paper." She picks up the paper scattered on her bench, folds it together, and flips it to Wooden. "Look at it. People don't come out and say they were attacked by vampires. They say they were hallucinating. They assume they were dreaming or having a psychotic episode. It's a psychological phenomenon--block out what you don't comprehend--what doesn't fit in with your basic assumptions about the world. But it's there, anyway. It shows up eventually."

Wooden looks at the paper. Buttonwillow has circled articles in red. He reads them aloud. "Man jumps from thirtieth floor", "Wife arrested for beating husband", "Businessman kills family, then self", "Seven car pile up on highway one-oh-one", "Woman destroys TV with hammer". He looks them over. Herman walks to the corner and reads over Wooden's shoulder.

Herman looks up. "So how do you know these have anything to do with the film? They seem like normal, everyday crime."

"First, the times. They all take place between eight forty-five and midnight. Second compare them to any other day. Maybe you'd have one or two of these that would be grotesque enough to make the paper. Last night--seventeen separate incidents. That's statistically significant. They're all connected."

"So you think . . ."

"I know. I also know how to stop it."

"Okay," says Wooden hesitantly. He looks at Buttonwillow. Her simple, flowing, flowered sack dress. Her soft hair, simply cut and lying plainly around her face and shoulders; her bright eyes and full smile. He can't help but think of her as a young girl--sweet and naive. But the seriousness of her words contrast strongly with her innocent appearance.

"This is some sort of voodoo type manifestation," she continues. "A spirit that died is still intertwined with a physical object in this dimension. That object, a film, has an essence of its own so that when that essence is transferred--in other words the film is projected or broadcast--the spirit is able to transfer a piece of itself with it."

Herman frowns impatiently. "Can you get to the part where you tell us what we have to do to stop it?"

"We have to destroy the original film."

Herman paces. "The original film? You mean the assembly cut or the rough cut or answer print or the first release print? What?"

"I mean the film that has the original image on it. The film that was in the camera."

"The negative."

"You know where that is?" asks Wooden.

"Should be in the vaults at Gigantus Films. I can't guarantee it. They're supposed to keep them there but who knows if someone moved it. This wasn't exactly a classic to keep for posterity." Herman turns to Buttonwillow. "So you know that destroying the negative will stop all these murders and all this weird shit going on."

"That's what I believe."

"You believe?" asks Herman. "So you don't really know."

"No, I don't, but this is my hypothesis--based on my research. And my education and experience."

"And if you're wrong?"

"If I'm wrong, then millions of people will die."

Wooden looks at her. "Millions of people?"

"You haven't read the TV section. It's on again tomorrow night."

"The movie? Again?" Herman clenches his good fist. "They wouldn't show it twice in a row. That wouldn't make sense. From a marketing point of view . . ."

"Well, they're doing it. On national TV this time."

Wooden rips through the newspaper in his hands looking for the television listing. He finds it, runs his finger down it, and lands on *Horror Flick*. He lets out a loud groan of exasperation.

Herman looks over Wooden's shoulder and also sees the listing. He brings his good hand up and presses the open palm against his face. He too groans, loud. Very loud. Wooden and Buttonwillow turn to look at him, his face frozen in horror and disgust. "Color? Oh, God. They've colorized my film."

After a moment, Wooden stands up. "Okay, here's what we do. Roger, can you get us into the Gigantus vaults?"

Roger Herman brings himself back from the verge of tears and straightens himself up. "Yeah. Yeah I can do that. They're at the corner of Mallover and Eucaliptus."

"Okay. It's got to be tonight. We'll go tonight. When's the best time?"

"Eight thirty is when the security guard shift changes. I'd say eight fifteen, eight thirty is the quietest time. Before the late shoots start dropping off equipment and film."

"Okay. We'll meet at eight at the side door of

Gigantus. On Mallover Street. You know where that is?"
Buttonwillow nods. "Now what do we need? How do we
destroy it?"

Buttonwillow shrugs. "That I don't know exactly. It
depends on the original incantations that were used. It depends
on which dimension the spirit is occupying."

"So what's our best chance. What do you
recommend?"

"Garlic and silver bullets?" asks Herman
sarcastically.

"Yes, that wouldn't be bad," replies Buttonwillow,
not catching the sarcasm. "Wooden stakes, crosses--really
symbols from any organized religion preferably over a few
centuries old--the newer ones generally don't have enough
spiritual preeminence."

"Are you serious or are you putting us on?"

"Mister Herman, if you want my help you're going
to have to go along with me!"

"Well, if that's the stuff you need, it's no problem.
I've made more horror films than any person alive. I'll just raid
one of my stock rooms. Why don't I just write this stuff down."
Herman takes out a pad and pen and begins writing.

"Good idea," says Wooden, "we'll make lists."

They gather around the table in the center of the room and list every possible weapon and deterrent they can think of. After twenty minutes they are finished and divide the procurement responsibilities among themselves.

"Good," says Wooden when they are all finished. "Gigantus Films. Eight o'clock. Side door on Mallover Street. Got it?"

"Got it," says Buttonwillow.

"Got it," says Herman, his head hung low. "I can't believe this."

Wooden comes over to him and puts an arm around Herman's shoulder. "We'll do what we can to stop it. That's the best we can do."

Herman nods slowly, unconvinced. Softly, "I can't believe it."

"It's hard for me to believe, too." says Wooden comfortingly.

"They colorized my film!"

Chapter 41

The Gigantus Films, Incorporated building is a full city block of windowless grey concrete. It stands like a looming monolith of stability and durability when in reality it houses one of the most fragile businesses these days--the movie business--and could crumble spontaneously, spiritually and financially if not physically, from the simple verbal onslaught of a disenchanted critic or an unresponsive public. Nonetheless it is an imposing structure, an anchor among the crumbling brick houses and rising iron-boned skyscrapers in this section of the city. The building's sides are dark but framed within thin silver lines along its edges from the glint of the full moon. The same moon also casts shadows that turn the sidewalk trees into skeletal claws which scratch upward at the concrete slab.

Brent Wooden stands as a speck next to this imposing structure, rubbing his hands together in the chill of an unseasonably cold evening. In his mouth, he sucks laboriously on a Gotu kola stick, his saliva and the potent flavor filling his mouth, mingling into a tangy serum that trickles down his throat to warm his stomach. Still he shivers, perhaps not so much from the unusual chill of the night air, but from an internal chill of his own cold thoughts and expectations.

Presently a chugging sound nears, and an old Volkswagen beetle hiccups around the corner into a parking space across the street. Buttonwillow McKittrick gets out, removes a red book bag from the back seat and swings it across her shoulder. She approaches Wooden, smiling, her step as bouncing and youthful as always. She is dressed in a white Victorian outfit, layered and frilled and extending down to her wrapped and sandaled feet. The layers of fabric still hide her body but swing to and fro, revealing moonlit glimpses of what Wooden sees as soft, fine curves unobstructed by any visible form of underclothing. The top of the dress reaches up to her neck in the back but falls over her shoulders and curves down low in front to reveal her 'ample bosom' pressed together firmly so that her cleavage appears to be the backside of an eager diver into her lower regions. Wooden pictures her without her clothes, her soft white skin caressed by moonlight, the ends of her fragile golden hair tickling the back of her neck. Her pouting, pale lips . . .

"Hello."

He puts her clothes back on her, and quickly swallows a pool of saliva and Gotu kola juice, a little of which enters his windpipe starting a violent coughing fit. He raises his hand until the coughing slows and he can catch his breath. "Hello," he says, then rubs his hands together briskly to heat them in front of his warm breath. "Herman's not here yet."

"Oh." She looks at him and winks. Wooden looks at her a little puzzled, a little embarrassed. Before he can say anything else, a red Porsche Carrera zips around the corner and screeches to a halt behind Buttonwillow's beetle. The door flings open and out bounds Roger Herman, unfolding himself from the little car to his full height. He stands for a moment smiling and at full attention in khaki fatigues, a pistol at his side, a knife strapped to his leg, a belt of silver bullets draped across one shoulder and an automatic weapon in his right hand. His left arm is still in a sling. Tucking the weapon into his sling he happily salutes his comrades on the sidewalk and runs over to the trunk from which he pulls an army green duffel bag which he throws over his shoulder.

"Roger Herman present and accounted for," says Herman still smiling.

"What are you doing, Herman? You have permits for this stuff? I could arrest you just for carrying it!"

"This is a war, Wooden. I've come here to destroy this monster and I'm not pulling punches. You've seen what it can do. If I could have strapped more guns, knifes, or automatic weapons to my body I would have."

"Well, you don't have to enjoy it so much. It's only . . ."

"Boys, boys," says Buttonwillow in her best grade school teacher tone. "If we're going to stop this thing we're going to have to be a team. Now please act like one." She reaches into her cleavage--Wooden's heart skips a few--and gently pulls out a small gold cross suspended on a fine chain around her neck. "I brought my religious symbol. How about you two?"

Wooden reaches around to his back pocket and takes out a wooden cross with the thin, tortured figure of Jesus nailed to it. "Will this do? It's been in my family for several generations."

"Good. Roger?"

Herman hesitates for a moment then unbuttons his shirt and lifts a gold chain from the thick curls on his barrel chest. At the end of the chain are two Hebrew letters. "I'm not sure if this'll work, but it's the best I could do." He holds it up and they look at it. "I'm Jewish . . . but I'm not really very religious." He pauses. "This is the Hebrew word 'chai'. It means life."

Buttonwillow looks at it curiously. "To tell the truth I'm not sure. That's not really a religious symbol, you know."

"Yeah, I know. I've also got this." He opens a shirt pocket and pulls out a small gold vial with delicate carvings on the side. "It's a mezuzah. I pulled it from the doorway to my house. It's got a prayer inside."

"Oh, that's good," says Buttonwillow encouragingly.

"And this." He unbuttons his other pocket and takes out a number of six-pointed Stars of David. "I sharpened the edges. Watch." He takes one in his hand and flicks it outward quickly and forcefully. It embeds itself in a tree. "A Jewish throwing star."

"Very good," says Buttonwillow.

"And this." Herman reaches into his duffel bag and pulls out an eight candle candlestick with metallic vines and leaves encircling it. "It's a menorah." Herman dances around waving the menorah in front of him.

"Good, good," says Buttonwillow, "I think you're covered."

Herman stops his waving and smiles, satisfied.

"What else is in the bag?" asks Wooden.

Herman opens the bag and peers in. "Wooden stakes, mirrors, crosses, more silver bullets."

"Well, I've also got holy water," says Wooden, pointing to a plastic bag lying by the wall. "Father Macauly has his doubts about my sanity."

"And I've got the garlic," says Buttonwillow. She reaches into her book bag and pulls out three wreaths of the stinking rose. She places one around her neck and tosses the other two to Wooden and Herman.

"Does this really work?" asks Wooden, frowning at

the wreath.

"We'll find out," replies Buttonwillow. They reluctantly throw the garlic around their necks as Buttonwillow rummages through her bag. "I've also got witches books, bibles--Old Testament and New, a Koran, a Torah, the teachings of Gautama Buddha, the Communist Manifesto, Dianetics, and Dale Carnegie's *How to Win Friends and Influence People*."

"I won't ask," says Herman.

Buttonwillow looks up at him. "Religion can be defined in many ways, Mister Herman. I'm just not taking any chances." She looks back down into her bag. "I've also got rosaries, an Egyptian ankh, a Buddha, an African elephant and a Japanese charm."

"How much do you have in that little bag, Miss Poppins? What about a gun?" asks Herman.

"I don't need one and I don't want one."

"What?"

"He's right, Buttonwillow," says Wooden. "You need protection."

"I've got protection, right here in my bag. Guns are too dangerous. I won't carry one."

"Too dangerous?" cries Herman. "This thing, this ghost or whatever, is pretty dangerous too. It kills people!"

"He's right Buttonwillow. I've got a gun. I'm sure Roger's got one he can spare."

"Excuse me gentlemen, but what we're dealing with is a spiritual entity. My protection is in my bag and it's more powerful than an exploding projectile or any material object for that matter. It's you who are in need protection. So if you don't mind, you can keep your steel and gunpowder phalluses to yourselves, thank you." Buttonwillow smiles sarcastically. Wooden and Herman look at each other. Herman unconsciously strokes the barrel of his automatic weapon.

"The question," says Wooden after a moment, "is how are we going to get into there," he points at the studio, "carrying these," he points to the bags, "and looking like this," he points at Herman. "Especially Rambo here."

"You've never been to a movie studio I see," says Herman. "This is the Neverland of dreams and make-believe. No problem. Just sprinkle some pixie dust and follow me." Herman throws his duffel bag over his shoulder and heads around the corner toward the main entrance. Buttonwillow and Wooden look at each other, shrug, and follow this rather militant and weighty Peter Pan.

At the front gate, Herman approaches the night guard, nearly asleep in his small tollbooth. The guard looks up.

"Night, Felix."

"Night, Mister Herman." The guard looks Herman up and down, then pokes his head out at Wooden and Buttonwillow who smile nervously. "What you workin' on tonight?"

"*Invasion of the Amazon Mutant Cheerleaders.*"

The guard raises his eyebrows and rubs his chin, nodding. Herman leans in and whispers to him. The guard continues nodding his head, watching Herman then slowly looking over at Buttonwillow, then back at Herman. A sly grin breaks the surface of his face, then explodes into a hearty, knee-slapping laugh. "Whoooeee, Mister Herman. That one I gotta see." He shakes his head in wonderment. Herman slaps the guard on the shoulder and enters the studio, motioning for the others to follow. The guard keeps smiling, watching the others enter. They look at him cautiously, expecting to be stopped at any moment. He just watches and smiles and shakes his head. As Buttonwillow passes, his grin grows and his head swings in disbelief.

Wooden scurries up to Herman walking confidently ahead of them. "What now?"

"Into the vaults," says Herman, pointing at the grey block before them. Wooden sees now that the grey concrete building is really G-shaped with several smaller buildings scattered inside the fortress walls. Lights attached to the walls above doorways form yellow, orange, and red cones of visibility within the darkness. While the area is mostly deserted, a few people wander through the fortress, none of them taking more than a passing notice of this strange Mod Squad.

As they approach, Wooden feels his nerve endings tingling and the muscles in his temples twitch annoyingly. His heart rate begins to climb as does his breathing. Approaching one corner, he hears a slight clanging noise. He looks around uneasily. The clanging grows louder. Herman seems not to notice, intent on reaching the vaults. Buttonwillow, behind them, seems distracted as she rubs her temples. The clanging grows louder. They reach a corner and a metal fist shoots out in front of Wooden's face. He quickly ducks and spins around, whipping out his gun at a fully armored medieval knight.

"Sorry about that," comes a muffled voice from

behind the faceplate. "Long night. I'm real stiff." The knight continues with his aerobics. Herman lets out a hearty laugh.

"You seem pretty happy for some reason." Wooden angrily stuffs his gun back in his holster. "I don't think you're taking this seriously. We're facing a killer."

"Mister Wooden. You don't understand. My whole life has been making other people's adventures. I grew up on Gene Autry, Roy Rogers, John Wayne, Humphrey Bogart. Later, I got a chance to write my own adventures. I even got a chance to direct some of my heroes, except they weren't really my heroes. My heroes were the guys they played on the screen. The guys who shot the bad guys, rescued the girl, and got the respect of the world. Now I'm the guy. I'm the hero. I didn't realize it until tonight, but this is my dream. I'm psyched. I'm pumped. I'm it!" Herman lets out a big, loud whoop.

Buttonwillow approaches, rubbing her temples. "Whoa."

"Our friend's call of the wild bother you?"

"No, it's not that. I'm honing in on something strong. Really strong."

"The film?"

"That or an incredible migraine."

"We must be on the right track." Herman leads the three of them at double time to a door. "Here we are," he announces. He enters and they follow. The door opens to a hallway of grey walls and black and white tiled floors. They walk down the hallway, passing countless doors, all alike, until they reach a set of elevators. Herman presses the button. They wait a short time before the doors open. Frankenstein's monster exits and Buttonwillow lets out a short gasp while Wooden begins a crouch, putting his hand on his holster. The monster nods and smiles courteously and passes them. "You two have got to relax," he says as they enter. Herman pushes a button and the elevator, along with Wooden's heart, sinks.

The elevator doors open onto a large door with a young guard stationed outside. Herman walks over to him. The others follow. "Roger Herman. I'm here to check on some footage."

The guard looks up, not knowledgeable of Herman or not impressed. Herman takes out his studio ID and shows it to the guard. The guard studies it then hands it back. "Sorry, Mister Herman, you'll have to come back tomorrow during regular hours."

"It's an emergency. I've got a film with a deadline,

and I need some stock footage tonight."

"You should've sent in a notice earlier." The guard pantomimes a sweeping examination of his desk and the papers on it. "I don't have any official notice here to let you in."

"Listen," says Herman, growing angry, "this is a big budget film. Big big budget! If I don't get in tonight, heads will fly and yours'll be the first!"

The guard shrugs.

Wooden steps forward and takes his police ID out of his wallet. "This is actually official police business. It's very important."

The guard looks at the ID and hands it back. "Look, mister, around here anyone can get any kind of ID. You know how many cop films they shoot in a single day? Besides, first it's an important film, now it's official police business. If you're police, you come back with a warrant, okay. Otherwise, outta here."

Wooden and Herman turn to Buttonwillow. "What do you want me to do?"

"Can't you cast a spell on him or something?" asks Herman. Buttonwillow frowns in annoyance. Herman sighs, suddenly spins around, then pulls his automatic weapon out of his sling and points it at the guard's head.

"Roger!" cries Wooden.

"Listen, buddy," says Herman to the guard, "this is an A-K Forty-Seven, the most powerful automatic weapon on the market, and it can blow your head clean off. Now I know what your thinkin'. Is this real or just a prop? Well, it's fuckin' real!" He turns and squeezes of a few shots that ferociously blast against the wall, tearing off large chunks of plaster and tile. The noise is deafening. Sparks fly and a cloud of smoke rises. He turns to point it again at the guard's head.

The guard, eyes bursting off his face, looks at Wooden who nods his head.

"Roger! What are you doing?"

"Listen, miss, we're here to save the world. I'm not going to let him or anyone else get in the way." Turning to the guard again, "The keys, please." The guard hands them over nervously.

"So what do we . . ."

"Tie him up. I've got twine and tape in my bag."

Wooden proceeds to tie up the guard and tape his mouth. Buttonwillow looks on, angry. Herman uses the keys to unlock the heavy metal doors and, with the AK47 still in his hand, pushes the doors open with his foot. He steps inside triumphantly, stuffs the weapon back into his sling, and beats his chest with his good hand, letting out a frightening Tarzan yell of victory.

Wooden rushes in. "What are you doing!"

"This is it! I think it knows we're here. I'm just telling it we're not afraid."

"Well I am. And if you were sane, you'd be too."

Buttonwillow walks in. "Listen, you chauvinistic, macho dick. What you did out there . . . unhhhh!" Buttonwillow bends over, her hand to her head.

Herman and Wooden in unison. "What is it?"

"It's here. And it's strong."

The door slams shut behind them with a resounding crash. It is black inside.

"Wait. I've got a flashlight in here." Herman puts down his duffel bag and fishes around in it.

"Quickly," says Buttonwillow.

"Yeah," says Wooden. "Quick there's something on my back. A spider!"

Herman finds the flashlight.

"Quick it's at my neck!" Wooden is slapping his

back over his shoulder but whatever it is keeps dodging his hand. "Quick! Quick!" It moves to the front of his neck.

Herman turns on the flashlight to see a disembodied hand curl its fingers around Wooden's neck and squeeze. Wooden grabs the stump of the hand and pulls, spinning himself around but not doing anything to lessen the hand's grip. Buttonwillow reaches out and also grabs the stump. Wooden starts coughing and gasping.

Buttonwillow: "Roger. The holy water."

Roger reaches into Wooden's bag and takes out a Perrier bottle filled with holy water. He unscrews the top and lashes the bottle out, splashing the water on Wooden, Buttonwillow, and the hand. Where the drops land on the disembodied hand's flesh, dark smoking holes form. The hand's fingers shoot straight out. Wooden and Buttonwillow let go and the hand drops to the ground, smoking. It is limp for a moment, then pops up and scampers away into the darkness.

Wooden massages his neck and suppresses an urge to cry. "Shit."

Herman looks after the hand. "*The Crawling Hand*. Herb Strock, Nineteen Sixty-Three, starring Alan Hale, Jr." He shivers.

"What?" asks Wooden.

"*The Crawling Hand.* An alien virus takes over an astronaut's hand. He kills himself but the hand makes it back to earth. Attacking people. Killing them. That's what that was."

"Yucch," says Wooden as he too shivers.

"It's just the beginning," says Buttonwillow. "We're not even close yet."

Chapter 42

"Mom. Mom. Can we have some more?"

"More milk?"

"And more cookies. Please?"

"All right, boys, I'll be there in a minute." Miriam
Walker assuredly hustles around the pristine kitchen, scooping
a batch of homemade butterscotch chip cookies onto a plate.
With one hand she takes the plate and with the other a large
container of pure, homogenized, vitamin D fortified, white
milk and scurries out into the living room. There, Roy Walker,
a round angelic little boy and Tommy Tutwiler, his skinny little

friend, sit quietly, their feet dangling off the edge of the couch. They look up at her, beaming enthusiastically at the treat she brings with her.

"Goody, goody," says Roy happily through a cookie filled mouth.

"Thank you Missus Walker," says Tommy shyly with only a slight touch of his lisp.

"What are you two boys watching," asks Mrs. Walker, rubbing her hands on her flowered apron.

"Some movie," says Roy.

"Supposed to be good for you," adds Tommy, and the two boys roll over giggling and kicking.

"You two smart guys. What'll I do with you?"

"What's going on Miriam?" Mr. Walker in his never-out-of-style grey cardigan comes into the room smoking his pipe. He carries little Amanda, the one year old, and hands her gently to Miriam who cradles her in her arms and coos.

"The boys are just being silly," says Miriam in between coos. "They won't tell me what they're watching."

"It's just a movie, Mom."

"Not one of those mushy ones with boys kissing girls, I hope." Mr. Walker gives the boys a knowing smile and they burst out giggling and rolling and kicking once more.

"Naw, Dad. It's just an old movie."

"It's a scary movie, Mister Walker."

"Well, not real scary. It's some kind of space movie."

"Space movie, huh." Mr. Walker sits on the armrest of the couch and shifts his pipe to the side of his mouth. "Kind of like Flash Gordon or Buck Rogers?"

"Who?" ask the boys in harmony.

"Just the spacemen of my day. Before Star Trek and Star Wars and all that. Why I remember in my day . . ."

On the television screen, a space ship looking suspiciously like a trash can lid wobbles warily across the horizon. The boys point and giggle some more. Mr. Walker readjusts his pipe and looks up at his wife.

"Miriam. How 'bout another tall glass of milk." He punches her playfully on the shoulder.

"Coming right up," she says as she floats off to the kitchen. Mr. Walker lets himself slide down onto the couch. The boys poke each other and giggle and roll and kick as young boys do.

Chapter 43

"This way." Buttonwillow points ahead to rows and rows of shelves of film reels. Herman aims his flashlight forward and they follow him, slowly and huddled together. Behind them, a single flare from Roger Herman's bag sputters fitfully, lighting the way back out.

"Hold on a minute," whispers Wooden. They all stop. He takes one step forward. The floor creaks. "What the . . ."

"What?" asks Buttonwillow.

"The floor--it's creaking."

"So?"

"So look down," says Wooden. Herman points his flashlight onto the floor. "It's concrete."

"Roger!" cries Buttonwillow. A huge black shadow lumbers up behind Herman. Before he can react, two black arms slam down onto Herman's large shoulders, hurling him to the ground. Wooden turns around. The flashlight falls and spins, throwing patches of light and dark in all directions. Wooden tears out his pistol and fires above Herman's fallen torso. There is a fierce growl, swallowed short, and then a loud thump and a metallic crunch. Wooden scrambles for the flashlight and aims it at Herman on the floor, lying face to face with . . .

"A gorilla with a TV on its head?" Wooden looks at the lifeless black fur and metal creature on the floor. Herman opens his eyes into the creature's faceplate. "What in the world are we fighting, here?"

Herman pulls himself up. Looking down, "Ro-Man." He steps back.

"Mister Herman, I consider myself an expert in all manner of the occult and yet even I'm not familiar with this . . . ahhh . . . Ro-Man."

"From *Robot Monster*. A Nineteen Fifty-Three Z grade movie. Phil Tucker, director. With a cast of unknowns. They don't get much worse than this. My stuff is Oscar® material in comparison. Though they did get Elmer Bernstein to do the score. Wish I knew how."

"Come on! This is a guy in an ape suit. This is stupid." Wooden reaches down over the fallen fur behemoth to pull off its mask or unzip its costume when something wet smacks into his face and wraps slender tentacles around his neck. He flies backward into a shelf of film reels and pulls at the thing on his face. Another one flies at Buttonwillow and attaches itself to her cleavage. Herman quickly reaches for her with his one good hand as Wooden struggles with the slimy thing slobbering down his face. He wrenches it off and slams it against a shelf. The grey tentacled thing bursts with a "sglurp", spraying gooky red slime onto Wooden's face and shirt.

Herman wrestles with the thing on Buttonwillow's bosom, finally pulling it off, throwing it to the ground, and stomping on it with his boot. A similar "sglurp" noise precedes a fountain of reddish goo as Herman's foot makes contact.

Another thing attaches to Wooden's leg and he sees now that it is a brain! A grey, football-sized brain with tentacles and antennae. Another flies out to cling to Herman's arm, which he smashes against a wall, splattering more goo.

"Down!" yells Herman with the commanding authority of a military officer or film director. Wooden falls to his knees as he wrestles with his brain. Buttonwillow slinks down along one of the racks. Herman, his flashlight and AK47 machine gun in the same hand, sprays the air in front and above them. Several dozen flying brain creatures burst and plummet to the floor in a pool of red slime. Wooden puts his fist through the creature that was attached to his leg and pulls it out, staring at it. Herman stops and steps back to catch his breath.

"What . . ."

"*Fiend Without a Face*, Nineteen Fifty-Eight. An Arthur Crabtree film with Marshall Thompson and Kim Parker."

Wooden, still staring at his slime drenched fist, leans over and vomits.

Buttonwillow examines the red stain on her white dress. She attempts to pull together the ripped neck of her already low cut dress, but stops trying and lets the flaps fall to reveal even more of her full chest. "I have to admit, I may be out of my league now. None of this makes sense to me."

"Then you're lucky I came along," says Herman. "This is all film stuff."

"So what is this? Are we trapped in a low budget horror film?"

"That's what it looks like."

Wooden leans upright and pulls his shirt tail out of his pants to wipe his mouth and then his hand. He feels the nausea sloshing around in his head. "What do we do now?"

"Keep on going," says Buttonwillow, stretching her neck to either side to crack it and remove the stiffness. "I can still sense the entity we're after. It's up ahead." She moves forward, followed by Herman and, slowly getting up, Wooden.

"Look up ahead," says Herman.

"Fog. Where'd that come from?" says Wooden. "All we need now is music." At that a loud organ note, so low pitched as to almost be inaudible, vibrates the floor, the shelves, and drills into their bones. They shudder. The music swells, reverberating through the building.

"Bach," whispers Herman.

"What?"

"Bach," repeats Herman over the music. "Toccata

and Fugue in d. *Phantom of the Opera*, Nineteen Forty-Three,

with Claude Rains."

They move on slowly through the mist, the three of

them, the concrete floor creaking beneath their steps, the organ

loud and ominous. Buttonwillow pulls out two books from her

book bag--a bible and Dale Carnegie--and holds them against

her chest. Herman keeps his AK47 at the ready, pointing in

front of them. Wooden steps cautiously, bringing up the rear,

his gun in one hand, a soda bottle of holy water in the other. He

peeks quickly into corners, to the side, and behind them.

Chapter 44

"Where you two think you're goin'?"

"Out. Cruisin'." Roberto Rodrigues defiantly pulls on his black leather jacket. Jesus Coronado looks at him then back to Mr. Rodrigues in the other room.

"Without a license?" calls Mr. Rodrigues.

"Who's gonna fuckin' know?" He jostles Jesus to hurry him out.

"Without car keys?"

"I got my own keys, you stupid . . ."

"Without a battery?"

Roberto stops and looks at Jesus then back at his father in the other room. "Aw, you fucker. You took out the battery."

Mr. Rodrigues calmly and haughtily brings his Budweiser® up to his mouth and sips slowly. The thick black hairs of his chest, like cultivated sprouts, poke out from under the gentle cotton wrap of his undershirt.

"You shit. You did that."

"No son o' mine is gonna end up in jail, you piss pot."

Roberto raises his fist threateningly and leans toward his father. Mr. Rodrigues looks up at his son, boldly, but leans away nonetheless. Jesus raises his own arm and puts his hand around Roberto's forearm, looking Roberto in the face. "Hey man."

He pauses for a moment, the three of them frozen. Jesus continues. "Be cool."

Roberto calms down and slowly brings his fist down to his side with Jesus's guidance. "So, Mister Rodrigues. What's all on the tube?"

Mr. Rodrigues settles back into the easy chair and empties his beer into his face. "A monster movie is all."

"Hey, man, a monster movie," says Jesus, beating playfully on Roberto's chest. "You like monster movies, yeah?"

"I'm not watchin' nothin' with this dirt bag."

Mr. Rodrigues turns to look at his son with an evil eye. Roberto returns it.

"Come on, man. Monster movie. Cool. Look, like with a big-titted chick, yeah? Monster movie, man. It's cool."

Roberto looks at Lieutenant Zimba on the TV screen. He plops down on the floor. Jesus slides down to join him. Jesus pokes him, smiling. "Monster movie. Cool, man."

Mrs. Rodrigues walks into the room carrying their little girl, wailing.

"Hey," shouts Mr. Rodrigues at his wife. "How about another beer." He holds up his empty can.

"Get it yourself, you bag of shit." Mrs. Rodrigues walks out. Mr. Rodrigues throws the can of beer after her which clanks against the wall and plinks on the ground.

Chapter 45

      Buttonwillow bites her lip, drawing a tiny trickle of blood. Small lines of perspiration meander down Roger Herman's forehead into his eyes, stinging. Wooden's lungs labor forcefully as his heart pounds in his ears. The mist is damp, like a steam room or a hot swamp, and the moisture permeates their hair and their clothes, gluing them to their bodies. It's a greasy wetness that beads up into little moist pearls that cling to their flesh and remain, suspended.

      "This is starting to look familiar," says Herman.

      "Familiar like how?" asks Wooden. "Like a familiar

movie?"

"No, like we're getting closer to where the film is stored."

"Yeah and this headache's getting worse," complains Buttonwillow, rubbing her temples. She stops and looks around. "This way." She points down a corridor of shelves. Herman takes another flare from his bag, lights it, and places it on the ground at the intersection of the two corridors. He points his flashlight down the one marked by Buttonwillow and they follow the yellow beam past rows and rows of film canisters and reels.

The Phantom's opera music has gradually faded and been replaced by something more contemporary. Not really music, it's a screeching, random arrangement of high pitched violin strings and tinkling metal bells.

"You hear something?" says Buttonwillow.

"You mean this . . . music? Is this from another B movie?"

"I don't recognize it," says Herman. "Could be background music from any run-of-the-mill horror film."

"Not the music," says Buttonwillow. "Something else."

"How can you tell?"

"Rustling or flapping."

"Bats?"

"Maybe."

"Above us?" Herman points the flashlight upward, searching the high ceiling for signs of life. Or death.

"Nothing," says Herman. "Maybe it's the music."

"Or the headache," adds Wooden.

They walk onward.

"There it is again," says Buttonwillow. "I heard something."

There is a rubbery, flapping sound.

"I heard it, too," says Wooden.

"Over here," shouts Buttonwillow. Herman swings the beam over to her then over to the shelf next to her. Sitting there is a grey rubber bat with big pincers at its mouth and great bubble eyes on the top of its head.

"It's just a rubber . . ." Wooden begins to say, but he sees the bulbous eye blink. He stops. Buttonwillow takes a step back. The rubber bat starts to launch itself off the shelf. Wooden, without conscious thought, pulls the crucifix from his back pocket, swings it over his head, and slams the point down into the creature's back just as it lifts off for flight. It is slammed back down onto the shelf, the point of the cross entering its body easily. Wooden brings his other hand around so that both are on the shaft of the crucifix, plunging it deeper as the rubber bat creature shakes and shudders violently, finally releasing a tiny screeching death scream before flopping down still. Wooden releases his hands. The cross, at an angle, remains embedded in the bat thing, Christ's feet standing on its back in triumph. Wooden steps back, bumping onto Buttonwillow.

"Take these," says Herman, handing the two of them lit flares from his duffel bag. "Hold them above your heads."

"What for?" asks Buttonwillow, complying.

"To keep them away," responds Herman. In the light of the flares they now see hundreds of rubber bats lining the tops of the shelves, an occasional wing fluttering or head bobbing or eye blinking. "Follow me. It's around here somewhere." He runs down the corridor.

"What? What's here?" asks Buttonwillow.

"It. *It Conquered the World*, Nineteen Fifty-Six, a Roger Corman film with Peter Graves and Lee Van Cleef."

"But what's *It* look like?" asks Wooden.

"Like . . . something like a giant eggplant."

"Eggplant?"

"With eyes and fangs and claws. We kill *It* and these bat things die, too," says Herman. "It also explains the power failure in here."

"It does?" asks Wooden.

"*It* sucks up power. In the movie, *It* can nullify power sources."

"Oh, well that explains it." Wooden rolls his eyes. "I don't mean to sound skeptical," says Wooden between huffing breaths, "but does any of this seem a little silly to anyone else. Apes in TV helmets, flying brains with tentacles, rubber bats, giant eggplants."

"There are more things in heaven and earth, Mister Wooden, than are dreamt of . . ." says Buttonwillow. Suddenly a dozen of the bats things swoop down on Buttonwillow. She swings at them with her flare.

"Keep the flare at them," shouts Herman.

"What's that?" shouts Wooden, as he takes off down the corridor toward a scuffling and banging noise. He rounds the corridor and facing him is none other than *It*, a giant, squat eggplant about six feet tall with Neanderthal brow, white carrot stick fangs, and large lobster claws. It scuffles along the cold, concrete floor toward him, its claws opening and closing, its long arms flailing mechanically. Wooden fires off shots, one at a time, emptying his gun into the thing. It continues at him, grinning.

Herman leaps around the corner. "It's bulletproof!" he shouts as he lunges at the creature with his flare. The monster bursts into flames and lashes out with its claws, throwing Wooden against a shelf. Wooden slumps to the ground and Herman grabs him and drags him out of the corridor.

"Of course," Wooden mutters to himself, "a bulletproof eggplant."

"Help!" screams Buttonwillow at the other end of the corridor. The Frankenstein monster is behind her, large and bulky with deep black stitches on lifeless pale skin. His hands grasp at her shoulders. She spins around and smashes the toe of her sandal into the monster's groin. Herman and Wooden, watching, both cringe and twist. The monster just grumbles and reaches for her face with one large, decaying hand. Buttonwillow slams her hand into his solar plexus, sending him backward one step before he regains his balance and lets out a sustained unpleasant grumble from deep in his chest. Reaching up, she puts a finger around one of his neck bolts and pulls his head down, slamming his nose with the palm of her other hand. The monster reels back.

In the meantime, Wooden quickly reloads his gun with the supply of silver bullets from Herman. Herman scrambles down the corridor, sliding to his duffel bag and pulling out an object. "Stand aside!" he yells and charges down the corridor. Buttonwillow sees him and spins around to run. The monster grabs one of her frills and tugs at her. She takes hold of a shelf and pulls. Herman runs at them both, building up speed. Wooden scrambles to his feet and follows Herman, his gun out. Buttonwillow braces her feet against the concrete floor and pushes off. The dress tears. She spins around, her spine hitting a metal support. Herman leaps at the Frankenstein monster, imbedding the menorah into its chest. The monster roars, falling backward, thrashing on the ground and wailing. Herman sails into the shelves bashing his flashlight against a metal rack. A film reel falls off, slamming into his shoulder.

The Frankenstein monster abruptly stops its thrashing and freezes. Wooden runs down the corridor. "Buttonwillow!" he calls out as a large, green, scaled and webbed hand curls slowly over Buttonwillow's mouth and pulls her quickly back between the racks. Wooden reaches the rack, his gun leading. He stops. Herman runs over to him. They look down the aisle between the racks. It is empty.

Chapter 46

"Hey, sailor, wanna have a good time?"

"Cut it out, Wendy."

Wendy straddles Albert in bed, her hands working their way down the front of her dress, leaving a trail of undone buttons. "Ta da da da, ta da da da . . ." she booms in her best strip tease music.

"Wen . . ."

She continues, "ta da da da!" She throws open her dress top to reveal her brassiere, then closes it quickly in mock embarrassment. She leans closer. "They've got your name on 'em. See." She leans closer and pulls open her dress top again. "Al," she says, nodding at her right breast. "Bert," she says nodding at her left. "Albert!"

"Not now, Wen" replies Albert.

"Not now?" repeats Wendy as she falls over next to Albert on the bed. "When?"

"Just not now."

Wendy pouts for a moment, then turns and puckers up her lips and places them next to Albert's cheek. "How a bout a kiss, then. Just a wee widdle kiss."

Albert turns and pecks Wendy on her over-puckered lips. She turns over, disappointed. "My Grammy gives me more passionate kisses than that."

"Not now, Wen. I had a hard day, today."

"Did you say hard?" Wendy's eyes light up mischievously as she reaches over and puts her hand on Albert's crotch. "You just said da magic woid," she says in her best Groucho, her free hand waving an imaginary cigar.

"I told you, Wen, I had a bad day. I'm tense."

"I know how to relieve tension."

"I have a headache."

"I know how to relieve a headache."

"And I'm tired."

Wendy takes her hand from Albert's groin and crosses both arms across her chest as she leans back against the pillow. She grumbles loudly.

Albert takes the remote control from the night table and turns on the television. He flips through a few stations. "Come on, Wen. Maybe there's something good on TV." He reaches for her hand but she pulls it away and turns her head from him. "Look here's that show about lawyers trying to jump into bed with each other."

Wendy harrumphs quietly.

He flips stations again. "Or the show with bartenders trying to sleep with each other."

No response.

"Or this show about bizarre Midwesterners trying to . . ." He flips some more and finally comes to Lieutenant Zimba receiving her orders and saluting her commanding officer. "Hey, an old sci-fi movie. How 'bout it?" He reaches out and pets Wendy's side. "Come on, Wen, you like these."

Wendy looks up at the screen. She frowns.

"Come on, Wen. We'll laugh. It'll be fun." Albert strokes Wendy's arm. She pulls it away.

"Screw you," she says, turning on her side and staring at the wall.

Albert continues watching the television, fascinated.

Chapter 47

Herman and Wooden trudge down the long, dark corridor, their hand held flares casting suspicious shadows on the walls.

"What happened to Buttonwillow?" asks Wooden, dejectedly.

"How the hell do I know?"

"Is she dead?"

"I told you I don't fucking know!"

"You act like you know. Every time something happens you reel off a name and date."

"I told you--everything has to do with some old B grade horror movie."

"Like apes wearing SONYs and rubber eggplants-- rubber *bulletproof* eggplants--with lobster claws and Frankenstein monsters. I'm the kind of guy that likes to reason through things. Go step by step and everything falls into place. Everything has a logical cause and effect. Well this stuff doesn't, and I don't know what to do with it. There's no rules here."

"There are rules. We just don't know them."

"Yeah, what rules have you figured out? What laws of physics haven't been broken in the last twenty minutes?" He pauses. "I mean, we're searching for this film, this holy grail. So what if we find it."

"We destroy it."

"And how do we know that'll stop the killings? Or the monsters?"

"Buttonwillow thought so."

The two men wander on in silence through the dim passages. The background music has stopped altogether. Even their footsteps no longer creak on the concrete. There is only silence. A death-like silence that is worse than the music.

"We'll get you, you son of a bitch," yells Wooden at the top of his lungs. It echoes along the metal rows, rattling the metal film canisters on them.

"Who?" asks Herman. "Get who?"

"Trantini. Or whoever is doing this. Whoever kill . . . kidnapped Buttonwillow."

There is more silence as the two men walk on. Suddenly, Herman shouts out, "We'll get you, you slime sucking shit hole, you!"

The two men listen to the tinny echo. Wooden looks at Herman, smiles and nods. "You mother fucking, amoebae-brained dirt ball!"

The two men laugh. "You're a maggoty, potato-headed, jello-dicked asshole!" shouts Herman followed by a loud whoop.

"And we're gonna crush your balls with a sledgehammer!" adds Wooden. Wooden stomps his feet on the ground.

"You're a fart-sniffing worm!" Herman begins dancing around, whooping like an Indian.

"We're gonna eat you up and shit you out!" Wooden and Herman exchange a high five and Wooden lets out a loud

"Hooooooey!"

Herman and Wooden start laughing hysterically until tears come out their eyes. "Flea shit . . . shoe" says Herman between coughs and laughs.

"Your penis . . ." gets out Wooden before his voice squeaks into nothingness.

The two men slap each other and dance and stomp and finally, gradually, the laughter and coughing and slapping and stomping subsides and the two of them lean back to catch their breath. After a few straggling chuckles are released, the two of them solemnly continue their journey, Herman examining the film can labels and Wooden examining the corners and shadows. After a moment, one of the metal racks shudders.

"What was that?" asks Wooden.

"Don't know." They continue walking. Another metal rack shudders. Wooden looks around nervously with his flare, seeing all sorts of horrors in the flickering shadows. Herman walks steadfastly forward, eyeing the titles on the films. Wooden slows to examine the shuddering shelves. The distance grows between them as Wooden holds his flare up to the shelves to peer into the crevices between film reels, trying to identify what might be behind them. Something moved! Or was it just a flickering shadow? There! Something else moved. Another shadow?

Wooden turns to see Herman farther down the corridor. He holds up his gun in a gesture as if to hail a cab. "Rog . . ." he calls when a hairy claw swings suddenly downward from the shelves to knock the gun out of his hand and down the corridor. Four small rivulets of blood stream down his slashed forearm. From the top of the shelves jumps down a werewolf who quickly grasps Wooden by the shoulders and pulls him forward. The werewolf's eye burn darkly into Wooden's. Wooden feels the heat of the werewolf's damp breath on his face as the lips curl to reveal massive sharp fangs. The werewolf growls a snarling threat and Wooden smells an odor of digested blood and flesh. Pressing inward, the werewolf raises Wooden in the air and easily tosses him backward to land painfully on his back. On his backpack, a broken piece of bottle glass cutting into his skin. The holy water seeping out onto the floor.

Herman turns to see the werewolf, but before he can react, he hears a screeching yapping sound from behind him. He turns back around as a large hairy dog charges him from the darkness and sinks its large teeth into his leg. He shakes his leg and the dog holds on, tearing the flesh in his calf. He brings his flare down. The dog holds on. He touches the flare to the dog's back and it opens its mouth and backs off, staring at Herman, not growling like a normal dog, but screeching at him. In fact it's not a dog at all, realizes Herman, but a shrew. Of course. A killer shrew. A mutant rodent the size of a dog.

Down the hallway comes the sound of legs on concrete. Rodent legs. Lots of them. Screeching loudly. A bizarre mutant cacophony. Herman alternately lashes his flare out to keep the one shrew at bay while using the same hand to try to get his AK47 out of his sling. The one shrew stands screeching. The other shrews approach cautiously. The blood seeps from Herman's torn pants leg and slices of flesh and denim dangle from it. The shrews are now visible, picking up velocity and running toward him at full speed.

The werewolf stands glaring at Wooden, gloating, its eyes radiating darkness. Its blood covered fangs bared, its blood covered claws outstretched. Wooden lies in a growing puddle of blood and holy water. His eyes have trouble focusing on the image in front of him. He takes the flare, still in his hand, and points it in front of him. The werewolf seems undisturbed and crouches on its powerful hind legs. Wooden moves the flare frantically in front of him. Next to him he sees his gun. The werewolf leaps.

Herman pulls his machine gun from his sling and fires off a frantic spray of bullets in front of him.

Wooden grabs his gun and fires upward.

The shrews falls into a large kicking, screeching pile. The werewolf lands next to him, dead. A few shrews, unharmed or simply wounded, run back into the darkness.

Herman hobbles over to Wooden. "You okay?"

Wooden struggles to get up. Herman tucks his weapon back into his sling and offers Wooden his hand. Wooden takes it and Herman pulls him to his feet. Wooden takes the backpack off and places it on the ground. Herman looks at the glistening gash on Wooden's back.

"How do you feel?" asks Herman.

Wooden glares at him.

"I mean, can you walk, can you move your arms?"

Wooden takes a few unsteady steps. He looks up at Herman and nods. "It's okay for now." He looks at Herman's shredded pants leg. "And you?"

Herman looks down then back up at Wooden. "Just a

flesh wound," he says with a forced smile. "The film's over here." He nods in the forward direction.

Through the darkness, a thin beam of light suddenly pierces the air ahead of them and crashes into a metal shelf. The shelf vaporizes into dark smoke as another beam spears the blackness and chars a reel of film on a shelf in front of them. Wooden backs against a shelf.

"What . . ." asks Wooden.

A large metal mass bursts from the dark mist in front of them. It is a robot of seamless silver skin with its head scraping the tall ceiling of the film vault. From the dark visor that masks its eyes shoots another narrow beam of light that blows chunks of concrete from the floor in front of them. Clouds of smoke and cement gush upwards.

"Gort!" says Herman. He pulls Wooden behind a shelf as another deadly beam chars the area they were just standing. This time, flames shoot upward to accompany the soot and smoke.

Herman wraps a large protective arm around Wooden. "*The Day The Earth Stood Still*, Nineteen Fifty-One. Directed by Robert Wise. A genius. Starring Michael Rennie and Patricia Neal. Great movie. I mean really great. A classic."

"Okay! So how do we stop it!"

"This one's easy. There's a command for the robot to stop."

The metal giant's feet scrape sharply against the floor as it turns the corner.

"Yeah?" asks Wooden.

"I'm thinking." Herman pauses. "I'm under a little pressure here."

The two of them stumble down the hallway. Gort reaches the opening and stands staring after the two of them. Wooden turns to look back, twists, and falls to the floor. He looks up at the behemoth who stares silently back, a small glow developing in its dark visor.

"What's the command?" yells Wooden. "What's the fucking . . ."

"I'm thinking!" yells back Herman. "Shut up! I'm thinking."

The glow in the robot's visor increases like a swirling yellow cloud as it builds up the energy for another laser blast. Wooden's sweat drips noisily onto the cold floor into little puddles. Herman inches backward slowly, his teeth chewing on his upper lip, his eyes, unfocused, darting in all directions. Herman whispers to himself. "Berrado. Bericto. Nada. Baricto nicto."

"The command!" shouts Wooden.

"Gort," shouts Herman suddenly at the metal behemoth. Did it stop for an instant? "Klaatu berada nicto. Klaatu berada nicto." The swirling yellow cloud continues for a moment. Gradually the swirling slows and the light fades. The giant brings its feet together to stand at attention and its visor slowly closes.

"Easy," says Herman. He smiles confidently as he takes Wooden by the arm. Wooden stares up at the frozen robot then back again at Herman. Herman leads them to another aisle. "It's here," says Herman as he wanders through the aisle. He comes to two indistinguishable dusty film reels and peers closer. He blows on them and a cloud of grey dust swirls back at him, revealing the faded typewritten labels. Herman points at it, happily. "This is it," he calls out to Wooden leaning wearily against a shelf. Wooden happens to glance up and notices a large glob of goo forming on the shelf above Herman. He stares at it. It grows as if someone were squeezing a giant tube of toothpaste gel. It creeps over the edge of the shelf when Wooden realizes its target--Herman.

"Roger!" yells Wooden as he runs down the aisle and throws himself at Herman, knocking them both out of the aisle and to the floor, Herman's AK47 clattering against the wall. A fist-sized glob drops where Herman was standing.

Herman looks at the goo. "*The Blob*, Nineteen Fifty-Eight with Steve McQueen," he explains when the rest of the sticky mass, a small dump truck load of goo, flops down over the shelf and completely fills the aisle. "And it's got the film. Damn!"

Floating around the corner comes a familiar Eastern European accent. "So now I suggest the game is over." Reva Trantini appears. With him is Buttonwillow. He has one hand over her mouth, the other on a laser gun pressed to her temple. Wooden brings his gun up quickly and centers Trantini's right eye squarely in his sight.

"Don't do it Mister Vooden. You see . . . I am not afraid of death."

Wooden holds his gun trained on Trantini. He thinks about the odds. He could blow Trantini away. But would that even kill him? Is he already dead? Could he still kill Buttonwillow? As he thinks all this, he realizes he has already lost his advantage. His arm is tiring and his nerves are unsteady as is his aim. He tries to keep Trantini in his gun sight, but his

eye begins clouding and his hand begins shaking and finally,

he drops the gun.

"Goot," responds Trantini and he takes his hand off

of Buttonwillow who steps quickly away. Trantini aims the gun

at Wooden. "I vouldn't have shot my own daughter anyvay,

you know," he says.

"Your daughter?" says Wooden.

"Your daughter?" says Herman.

"Your daughter?" says Buttonwillow.

"Yes, my daughter," says Trantini. He stands before

them, his black cape blowing restlessly behind him in the

windless vault. He is all black and white. His jacket: dark

black. His shirt: bright white. His hair: jet black. His face:

deathly pale white. His eyes: limitless black. "Yes," he

continues. He turns to Buttonwillow. "Your mother and I were

more than good friends, my dear. I have a place in my heart for

her. She taught me to escape. She tried to teach me to love. I

don't know . . . some lessons are more difficult than others."

"To escape?" asks Buttonwillow.

"To escape from life. From death. To escape from

this vorld of three or four dimensions into other places, other dimensions. Afterlifes. Beforelifes. Vhat ve live in is only a small part of existence." He looks at the confused expressions on Wooden's and Herman's faces.

"You escaped your death by extricating your essence into another dimension at the moment that your essence died in this dimension," says Buttonwillow for clarification.

"Yes. You understand. You have your mother's intuition." Trantini looks Buttonwillow up and down slowly with a smile.

"Okay, okay, so you sucked yourself into another dimension," says Wooden. "So why the killings? Why the gruesome murders?"

Trantini brings his attention to Wooden. All of Trantini's movements seem to be in slow motion, as if he were the master of time and he makes the clock move to his pace rather than being forced to race against it like others. "I can't give you a lesson in metaphysics, Mister Vooden. You vouldn't understand anyway." He turns to Buttonwillow. "There must be a balance, you know. Each time I visit this dimension I must compensate by sending others into another dimension. There are vays to do this, of course, but the easiest is by killing them. And you know, death is really not so bad.

Only a little boring. Which is vhy I made each killing particularly interesting. I am getting even more skillful, I believe." Trantini nods and smiles at his own ingenuity.

"And you!" shouts Trantini suddenly, turning and pointing at Herman. "Had you been a better director--more talented, more skillful--I vouldn't have had to vait so long. I had to find vays to communicate through the dimensions to get zat lousy moofie into video stores and on television. Didn't you ever vonder vhy a great film star vould agree to appear in a piece of crap such as *Horror Flick*." He pronounces the film title with loathing. "Finally, tonight it is being shown nationally. In only minutes . . ."

"Tonight?" says Herman. "It's on tomorrow night."

"Tonight!" shouts Trantini raising his ray gun at Herman. He calms down. "I got it moved up a night."

"You what?" says Herman. "With all my clout I couldn't get network TV to rearrange a schedule. You expect me to believe . . ."

"Mister Herman!" Trantini's eyes blaze, then as quickly he becomes quiet spoken and even tempered again. "I have powers beyond what you can imagine. For me, getting a network to rearrange its schedule is child's play."

Herman gasps in awe.

"But you, my child." Trantini says leering at Buttonwillow, "You are beautiful. I am proud that you are mine. You fill my heart vith . . . pride."

Buttonwillow looks at Trantini, puzzled, then smiles shyly and nodding.

"You are even prettier . . . and more capable than your mother. That is a compliment!"

Buttonwillow smiles again. She inches over toward the wall.

"I vould like you to join me, dear. Father und daughter. I can teach you to escape vith me. To visit other vorlds. To explore other dimension and planes. To visit with other spirits. Great spirits."

Buttonwillow still smiling inches closer to the wall. Wooden watches her. Herman is still contemplating the ability to get a network to rearrange its schedule.

"And you, my lovely, lovely, lady," continues Trantini perhaps blushing slightly, "you can teach me love." Trantini winks and smiles at Buttonwillow. Buttonwillow coyly smiles back and eases against the wall.

"Hey you old snot bag!" yells Wooden abruptly.

Trantini spins toward him, raises his laser gun, and presses on the trigger.

Buttonwillow pulls the AK47 off the floor and brings it up with her finger wrapped around the trigger. A spray of bullets punches a perforated line into Trantini from his crotch to his head as he flies backward against the wall. His laser gun beam cuts a yellow line into the air.

"That's gross," says Buttonwillow dropping her weapon like a leaking bag of garbage. "Can you imagine? Me and him." she says, turning to Wooden who shakes his head. "I mean, just what kind of guys did my mom hang out with anyway."

Wooden approaches her and they look at Trantini's body pinned to the wall, eyes wide and still staring hauntingly at them. Wooden shudders. "Is he dead?"

"Dead is relative, Mister Wooden. I would think you'd know that by now."

"Okay. Is he relatively dead? I mean can he do damage?"

"Truth is--I don't know. I would guess . . ."

A rumble begins in the vault. Film shelves begin shaking. All of them. Increasingly more violently.

"What's that?" asks Herman. A roar starts growing louder. They shout to speak above it.

"I think it's him," shouts Buttonwillow. "He's still manifested here." She stumbles and begins to fall, then catches herself. The floor is now shaking and bits of concrete are flaking off the walls and ceilings. Buttonwillow points at the Blob covered shelf. "We have to destroy the film!"

"How?" shouts Wooden.

"With this," shouts Herman. He reaches into a pocket and produces a hand grenade. "Get ready to run!" Herman pulls the pin. Buttonwillow and Wooden look at each other and take off down the corridor in the direction of the entrance. Film racks are falling to the ground. Bigger chunks of concrete are raining down from the walls and ceiling. Herman removes the pin of the grenade and tosses the grenade into the Blob by the film, which slowly sucks it in. Herman takes off down the corridor. He catches up with Wooden and Buttonwillow who are slowed by a shelf which has just crashed down in front of them. The three jump over the shelf, landing on the other side as a piece of ceiling smashes down behind them raising a small typhoon of choking dust. They continue running.

"I wish you'd given us more time before you pulled that . . ." Wooden's sentence goes unfinished as the explosion rips apart the shelves in the immediate area and the percussion knocks the three of them to the floor.

Chapter 48

Wooden struggles to pull his eyelids open. A wavy vision appears. Everything is white. A bright light surrounds him. He's in a tunnel. There's a strong bright light at the end. He's dead. Or dying. He opens his eyes wider to see the end. The destination. The answers to the universe. The final peace. Whatever it may be. He opens his eyes wider and tries to focus.

Buttonwillow stands looking out the window through which the bright sunlight of a beautiful day streams in. Herman sits on a chair thumbing through a copy of People magazine.

"I think he's awake," says Buttonwillow and then turns to confirm her statement. She comes toward him and Wooden sees her crutches. Herman looks up, puts the magazine down and comes over to him also.

"I had a dream," says Wooden opening his eyes to see that he is in a hospital bed. "And you were in it and you . . . and where's little Toto?"

"This isn't Kansas, Dorothy," says Herman smiling.

"So what happened?" asks Wooden.

"Starting when?" asks Buttonwillow.

"Starting with the grenade exploding."

"Everything went boom," says Herman. "We fell to the ground. Everybody got hurt--you the worst with some broken ribs, broken leg, lots of cuts and bruises, and a concussion. Me with a gnawed leg and a broken pinky." He holds up his pinky to show the splint. "And Miss McKittrick here with only a sprained ankle."

"Second degree sprain," says Buttonwillow indignantly and holding her crutches out.

"And then?" asks Wooden.

"And then," continues Buttonwillow, "the studio guards finally broke open the door and we're charged with a long list of crimes . . ."

"Which my lawyers feel won't be a problem--
especially since we were on official police business, right?"

"Well . . ." Wooden clears his throat. "What about
Trantini?"

"He's dead." says Buttonwillow.

"Yeah, but is he dead dead or living dead or undead
or what?"

"I mean he's gone from here. That's all I can tell. I
couldn't feel his presence any more. After the grenade
exploded. Suddenly the headache went away. Everything else
hurt, but my head was fine."

"And the people. The viewers. Did any of them . . .
did we save them?"

"No reports of any deaths so far," replies Herman.
"Lots and lots of weird incidents. You ought to read today's
paper." He picks up the paper from a table, looks at it, then
puts it down. "Then again, maybe not. Anyway, the world is
safe for now."

"It's amazing," says Wooden. "All that power. The
power to kill."

"The power to conjure all those spirits and other

world entities," says Buttonwillow.

"The power to rearrange network schedules," says Herman. They all pause to contemplate. "Anyway," says Herman, the first to snap out of his reverie, "I'm glad it's over; I'm glad we're all okay. I'm going home for some rest and to start production on a new film. I have this idea about a movie that's so bad, people die watching it."

Buttonwillow and Wooden turn to give Herman a sneer.

"Well, it's not exactly what happened to us. It's different. Look, any time I can make a bad experience into a profit, what's wrong with that?" They continue sneering at him. "Well, I'll think about it, anyway."

"I've got to go, too," says Buttonwillow turning back to Wooden. "I'm glad you're okay." She takes her crutches out from under her arms and clasps them together at her side. She leans over and kisses Wooden on the forehead, the loose neck of her flowered dress falling open in front of him. Yup, no underwear, thinks Wooden. Buttonwillow giggles. Whoa! Gotta watch what I'm thinking around this woman.

The two visitors gather together at the hospital room

door to leave. Herman waves. Buttonwillow smiles and winks.

Wooden falls comfortably asleep.